Badass
GRATITUDE

Enjoy *Badass Gratitude* as an audiobook, wherever audiobooks are sold.

Badass GRATITUDE

Affirmations for Slaying Your Way to Contentment

BECCA ANDERSON

author of *Badass Affirmations*

The authorised representative in the EEA is Simon and Schuster Netherlands BV, Herculesplein 96 3584 AA Utrecht, Netherlands. (info@simonandschuster.nl)

Andrews McMeel Publishing
a division of Andrews McMeel Universal
1130 Walnut Street, Kansas City, Missouri 64106

www.andrewsmcmeel.com

26 27 28 29 30 POA 10 9 8 7 6 5 4 3 2 1

ISBN: 979-8-8816-0218-5

Library of Congress Control Number: 2025945435

Editor: Kate Zimmermann
Art Director/Designer: Julie Barnes
Production Editor: Julie Railsback
Production Manager: Julie Skalla

To my mother Helen who is an exemplar
of the power of gratitude. Love. Eternal!

CONTENTS

INTRODUCTION

This Is Not Your Grandmother's Gratitude Book

(but She'll Like It Too)

Badass women inspired me, starting with the badass women in my family, an amazing first-grade teacher, and beloved friends. How can you tell a badass woman from the rest? She is the one who is "extra" and who puts in the work, the effort, the love, and takes the risks. She walks into the room and doesn't take up all the oxygen—instead, she breathes life into it. Want to see a badass woman in action? Look in the mirror!

As a badass woman, you're already a force, and thinking like a badass with a grateful heart? That's your secret superpower! Gratitude fuels a positive mindset, grounding you in joy while propelling you toward your dreams. Let's dive into how to think like a badass with kindness, optimism, and a heart full of thanks.

Gratitude starts with celebrating *you*. Take a moment to appreciate your strength—those times you pushed through doubt, juggled life's chaos, or lifted someone else up. Thinking like a badass means saying, "I'm thankful for my resilience." This isn't just feel-good fluff; studies show gratitude boosts self-esteem, making you chase goals more boldly. Write down one thing daily you love about yourself—it's like a hug from your heart.

Next, embrace gratitude for your journey. Every step—triumphs, stumbles, all of it—has shaped your brilliance. A grateful heart sees setbacks as lessons wrapped in love. Lost a job? You're thankful for the skills you gained. Tough day? You're grateful for the chance to grow stronger. This mindset shifts your thoughts from "Why me?" to "What's next?"—and that's pure badassery.

Thinking like a badass also means gratitude for your people. Your friends, family, or that stranger who smiled at you—they're your cheerleaders. Thank them in your heart or out loud. Research continues to find that gratitude for relationships sparks positivity, fueling the courage to take risks. Surround yourself with those who see your sparkle, and let their love remind you to think big.

How to Use This Book

Here is something that's going to light up your journey to awesomeness: Every chapter in *Badass Gratitude* is packed with little power hubs—mini-sections I've lovingly named "Affirmation Stations." Each one's loaded with affirmation examples to help you kick-start your path to becoming the most radiant, unstoppable version of you.

Here's the thing: affirmations aren't one-size-fits-all, and that's the magic of it! They're all about your dreams and your heart. Let's say you're craving a life of joyful independence—don't go saying, "I will love my partner well." Instead, try this on for size: "I am happy and so excited to be independent." Or maybe you're ready to shake things up in your career or land a new gig. Skip the "I am happy at my job" vibe and go for "I am capable of making positive changes." See the difference? It's all about speaking your truth, your way.

Here's a little tip to make these affirmations pop: Grab some highlighters or colorful pens (you know, the ones that make you smile), and mark the affirmations that feel like they were written just for you. Then, snag some sticky notes in your favorite shade—maybe a sunny yellow or a calming lavender—and jot down those affirmations. Stick them where you'll see them every day: your bathroom mirror, the edge of your laptop screen, or even your fridge door. These little bursts of positivity will be your daily cheerleaders, reminding you of your goals and your strength.

Keep *Badass Gratitude* somewhere you pass by all the time—like your nightstand or coffee table—so you can flip it open whenever you need a fresh dose of inspiration. As your dreams grow and evolve (just like you do), you can swap in new affirmations that match the incredible person you're becoming. You've got this, and I'm cheering you on every step of the way!

CHAPTER 1

How Gratitude and Affirmations Work

"Appreciation can make a day—even change a life. Your willingness to put it into words is all that is necessary."

—Margaret Elizabeth Cousins,
Irish-Indian educationist and suffragist

Gratitude is one of the loveliest paths to personal growth. It can be subtle; after contemplating what it is to be thankful, you may find that you have the "half-full mindset." Maybe instead of Sunday nights of worrying about work, meetings, and goals, you relax and remember to be grateful for the work you enjoy. Next thing you know, your coworkers pick up on the fact that you are less stressed out and more fun to be around, and your desk becomes an oasis of positivity in the office—people leave your workspace with a spring in their step. Your family responds in kind; and your home is a calmer, happier place filled with calmer, happier people. Your friends who used to call or message you and complain about life now call and tell you all the good things happening. That one took a while, but your aura of gratefulness eventually took hold and bloomed.

You, my friend, have an attitude of gratitude and are making the world a better place.

Well done, and please allow me to be the first to thank you. I guarantee you that I won't be the last. I am a big one for setting intentions and do so every morning. I intend for you to grow and soar in your wisdom; and all the better if some of the ideas, affirmations, practices, and suggestions included in this book inspire you.

Affirmations Can Heal a Broken Heart

You might imagine that I grew up in a home brimming with jollity, good humor, and thankfulness. The truth is that it was quite the opposite. My mother is a wonderful and generous person, but she carries a decades-long sadness that spilled over to the household, and it was palpable. It is also quite understandable. My mom was a fantastic student, and her future at college looked very bright. However, as she neared graduation, a mysterious malady affecting her mother was finally diagnosed as a rare blood cancer. There was no discussion about it; it was instantly understood that my brilliant mother would stay home and become a full-time caregiver. And, to her credit, she wasn't even thinking about that, only the well-being of her beloved mother. Unfortunately, the treatments for this condition were not nearly as advanced as they are now, and my grandmother suffered enormous pain and discomfort. She would cry out in agony and, in the last months of her life, take it out on my mother verbally. She told her she was ugly, stupid, that nobody wanted her. And much more. Her mother had become a veritable stranger because of her illness and a kind of dementia brought on by pain. Imagine being a teenager whose future evaporated after one visit with a doctor, and suddenly, your every waking moment is spent with a stranger hurling invective at you. It was simply soul-crushing for my mom. Her sense of self was scrambled, and her heart was broken. After the nightmare passage to her mother's death, my mom entered the workforce where, of course, she was the best at whatever she did. But the hole in her heart remained deep and wide. She later told me that only by having daughters of her own could she start to repair the void of love she felt.

My mom is beautiful both inside and out. She was the reason I started using affirmations because she had very low self-esteem because of her mother's illness. The work of her lifetime has been to heal her broken heart. Affirmations are a potent form of self-care, and I cannot recommend them to you enough. Heal thyself! One of the proudest moments in my life was when I gave my mom a finished copy of *Badass Affirmations*. She keeps it on her nightstand and affirms her worth every morning.

AFFIRMATION STATION

I am enough, in and of myself.

I am free from comparisons to the past.

I am happy for others and
happy with myself.

Power Up with Affirmations: How and Why They Work

Why do affirmations work? Because they're like planting seeds in the garden of your mind, and you, my friend, are the badass gardener. Affirmations aren't just fluffy words—they're intentional, powerful statements that rewire how you see yourself and the world. When you repeat them with belief, you're training your brain to focus on possibility, strength, and gratitude, drowning out the noise of doubt and fear. You don't need to be perfect; you just need to start. Speak your truth, even if your voice shakes at first. With every affirmation, you're building a stronger, kinder relationship with yourself—and that's where the real transformation begins. You've got this, and the universe is cheering you on.

The Science Behind Affirmations

Affirmations work because your brain is a malleable masterpiece, constantly reshaping itself through neuroplasticity. When you repeat positive statements like "I am capable," you're forging new neural pathways, strengthening connections that align with confidence and resilience. Research, including studies from Carnegie Mellon University, shows that self-affirmations can lower stress and boost problem-solving under pressure by activating the brain's reward centers, like the ventral striatum. This rewiring helps counter negative self-talk, which often stems from the amygdala's fear response. By consistently affirming, you train your prefrontal cortex—the part of your brain tied to decision-making and self-control—to prioritize empowering beliefs. It's like updating your mental software. Affirmations also influence your reticular activating system (RAS), the brain's filter for what you notice. Say "I attract opportunities," and your RAS starts spotlighting possibilities you might've missed. The key? Emotion and repetition. Feeling the words amplifies their impact, as shown in fMRI studies where emotional engagement lights up neural networks. Affirmations aren't just words—they're a science-backed tool to reshape your mindset, reduce anxiety, and unlock your inner badass, one intentional thought at a time.

Tips to Get the Most Personal Benefit from Affirmations

- Craft affirmations with self-care in mind: Use statements like "I prioritize my peace and well-being" to reinforce boundaries and nurture your mental health daily.
- Boost your self-esteem with personal truths: Choose affirmations like "I am worthy just as I am" to build unshakable confidence and silence your inner critic.

- Align with your goals: Create specific affirmations, such as "I take bold steps toward my dreams," to keep your focus sharp and motivation high.
- Infuse gratitude for deeper impact: Pair affirmations with gratitude, like "I am thankful for my strength and growth," to amplify positivity and emotional connection.
- Practice consistently with feeling: Say affirmations morning or night, five to ten minutes daily, with heart—feel the words rewire your brain and transform your mindset.

You Have to Think Badass to Be Badass!

Hey, you! Ready to unleash your inner badass? It all starts in your head—because to *be* badass, you've gotta *think* badass. Your mindset is the spark that ignites action, turning dreams into reality. Badasses don't wait for permission or perfect conditions; they cultivate a mental game so strong it powers through obstacles like a freight train. Let's break down how thinking badass fuels your unstoppable vibe.

First, badass thinking is about owning your power. It's believing you're capable, even when the world screams messages of doubt. Picture this: Every time you face a challenge, your brain's shouting, "I got this!" That's not arrogance—it's confidence rooted in self-trust. You're not faking it; you're building it. Each time you choose courage over fear, you're wiring your brain for resilience. Science backs this—positive self-talk rewires neural pathways, making bold actions feel natural over time.

Next, it's about vision. Badasses don't just think about today; they see the big picture. They dream audacious goals and reverse engineer the steps to get there. Your thoughts are a blueprint—make them epic. Visualize crushing that presentation, launching that side hustle, or nailing that workout. When your mind's locked on success, your actions follow suit.

But here's the real talk: Badass thinking isn't blind optimism. It's gritty. You acknowledge setbacks, but instead of wallowing, you think, "What's the lesson here?" Failure? Just feedback. Badasses reframe every stumble as a chance to level up. This mental agility keeps you moving forward, no matter what.

Finally, thinking badass means surrounding yourself with the right vibes. Your thoughts are shaped by what you consume—books, podcasts, people. Feed your mind with stories of triumph, ideas that challenge you, and individuals who lift you higher. Ditch the naysayers; they cause mental clutter.

Here's the kicker: Thinking badass isn't a one-time gig. It's a daily flex. Wake up, choose boldness, and act on it. Small wins stack up, turning your mindset into a habit.

Before you know it, you're not just *thinking* badass—you're *living* it. So start today. Tell yourself you're unstoppable. Take one bold step. Your thoughts are the fuel; let 'em roar.

"I don't have to chase extraordinary moments to find happiness—it's right in front of me if I'm paying attention and practicing gratitude."

—Brené Brown, American professor, social worker, author, and podcast host

Awesome Ways to Think Badass

MASTER YOUR SELF-TALK: Swap "I can't" for "I'll figure it out" by writing three affirmations daily—like "I'm fearless" or "I crush challenges." Say them out loud. Research shows that positive self-talk boosts confidence and reduces stress. Your brain believes what you repeat, so make it empowering.

VISUALIZE YOUR WINS: Spend five minutes daily picturing your success—vividly. See yourself acing that goal, feeling the rush. Visualization primes your brain for action, making goals feel attainable. Athletes use this to boost performance; you can too. Make your mental movie epic and watch your confidence soar.

LEARN FROM SETBACKS: When things go south, ask, "What's the takeaway?" Write down one lesson per failure. This reframes setbacks as growth fuel. Studies show that reflective thinking builds resilience. Badasses don't dwell—they dissect, adapt, and charge forward. Turn every stumble into a stepping stone.

CURATE YOUR INPUTS: Surround yourself with inspiration—podcasts, books, or people who spark boldness. Limit time with negative influences. Your mind absorbs what's around you, so choose wisely. A 2023 study found that positive social circles boost motivation. Feed your brain badass energy and watch your thoughts transform.

Claim Your Happy Place

"Just stay positive!" We are all told this countless times throughout our lives. It is easier said than done, but it is essential to maintaining a healthy lifestyle and supporting your well-being. It is very easy to get caught up in the difficulties we face daily. And while we need to face these in whatever manner we can, living a life of positivity is one of the best ways.

It may be as simple as flipping the script: Don't think of it as "I have to remain positive today." Think of it as finding ways to spread joy and happiness to those around you. Positivity is a powerful force that can make a huge difference to you and those you love. Look at your life and find ways to spin things in a better direction: Are you giving to others, or are you a little out of balance, where your work and immediate family get 99 percent of what you offer the world? You can change that in one day. Donate more of your time or money to a charity. Supporting a cause will help keep you informed about social issues and can strengthen your sense of well-being while benefiting others in the process.

Bringing joy to others is one of the best and most beautiful ways to create more positivity in your life. Being a source of happiness in another person's day can be extremely rewarding. To put this into practice, try thinking of how someone has turned your bad day into a joyful one. Did you receive a text from a friend or family member that instantly made you feel better? Was there someone who helped you with a work task that felt overwhelming? Take these small (but important) things, and find ways to give back that positivity. There are many ways you can plant the seed of happiness today—whether it be wishing someone a great day, complimenting someone's talents, or helping someone without being asked. You never know how much another person may need it. Scatter the seeds of happiness wherever you go, and watch them grow!

Sloughing Toward Gratitude

This might come as a surprise, but gratefulness did not come naturally to me. I was the youngest in a family of three, and I arrived late to the party, five and seven years after my two sisters. They were not exactly thrilled at my addition and made that clear to me, very loudly. Aside from my shy and quiet mom and me, we were a loud family: lots of piano playing, singing, laughing, and records playing at top volume. I just wanted to disappear, and when I was old enough to explore the family farm and what was to become my beloved woods, I was pretty good at it. Like many of you, I felt like I didn't fit in with my own family. It was not that comfortable. So I excused myself from family dinners as soon as I thought I could make a break and avoided the merry doings of my two older sisters, who were a tight unit. Now, of course, I can see their point of view—who wants the weird little sister around? Only when I went to school and experienced bullying in grade school, and my sister Marty defended me against a bully, was I really able to appreciate my sister and her loudness. I remember feeling proud of my sister, who was very talented and very pretty, and how easily she took care of business. I was enormously grateful that she came to my rescue, and I also took note of how to respond to rudeness and meanness. I saw a wonderful tenderness in my self-sufficient, cool older sister, and she and I became buddies. I stopped being scared of my own shadow that day. If my shadow started giving me a hard time, just wait until my sister straightened my shadow out!

I grew a little braver—and more grateful—that day.

BADASS PRACTICE: THE FAMILY GRATITUDE LOVE CHAIN

Gratitude in relationships isn't about ignoring the messy stuff—it's about seeing the love beneath it. It's thanking your mom for her late-night advice, your sibling for making you laugh, or your cousin for just being there. These small acts of appreciation can heal old wounds and make your family stronger. Pick a family member each week to focus on. Write down one thing you're grateful for about them—like "I'm thankful for Dad's silly jokes." Share it with them in person, over a call, or in a note. Then, ask them to share something they're grateful for about another family member. Keep the chain going, spreading gratitude through your family like a warm wave. You'll feel the love grow with every "Thank you."

Your family is your roots, and gratitude helps them grow deeper. Who will you thank in your family today?

How to Have an Attitude of Gratitude

1. Be grateful, and recognize the things others have done to help you.
2. When you say "Thank you" to someone, it signals what you appreciate and why you appreciate it.
3. Post a "Thank you to all" on your Facebook page or blog; or send individual emails to friends, family, or colleagues.
4. Send handwritten thank-you notes. These are special because so few of us take the time to write and mail them.
5. Think thoughts of gratitude—two or three good things that happened today—and notice calm settle in your head, at least for a moment. It activates a part of the brain that floods the body with endorphins, or feel-good hormones.
6. Remember the ways your life has been made easier or better because of others' efforts. Be aware of and acknowledge the good things, large and small, going on around you.

7. Keep a gratitude journal to list the people or things you're grateful for today. The list may start out short, but it will grow as you notice more of the good things around you.

8. Being grateful shakes you out of self-absorption and helps you recognize those who've done wonderful things for you. Expressing that gratitude continues to draw those people into your sphere.

9. Remember this thought from Maya Angelou: "When you learn, teach; when you get, give."

10. Join forces to do good. If you have survived illness or loss, you may want to reach out to others to help as a way of showing gratitude for those who reached out to you.

AFFIRMATION STATION

I am open to seeing the best of others at any time.

I can match that with my best.

Be inspired by the best everyone has to offer.

"The more you praise and celebrate your life, the more there is in life to celebrate."

—Oprah Winfrey, TV host, actress, businesswoman, author, and producer

The Power of "Thank You"

Let's talk about a heartwarming secret to a joyful, thriving life: gratitude for others. When you pour appreciation into the people around you, you're not just spreading kindness—you're building a foundation for happiness and success. With a grateful heart, you transform everyday moments into connections that lift everyone higher. Here's why appreciating others is pure magic and how to make it your superpower, all wrapped in upbeat, practical inspiration.

Gratitude for others is like a warm hug you give and receive at the same time. When you notice someone's effort—your coworker's knack for brightening the office or your neighbor's cheerful wave—it's a chance to shine light on their goodness. A simple "You make every day better!" can spark joy that ripples outward. Science agrees. Studies show that expressing appreciation boosts oxytocin, fostering trust and bonding. By saying, "I'm so grateful for your creativity," you're not just boosting someone's confidence; you're weaving a web of positivity that makes life sweeter. This habit turns strangers into allies and friends into family, creating a support network that fuels your success.

Why does this lead to a happy life? Because gratitude shifts your lens. Instead of dwelling on what's missing, you celebrate what's present—the barista's smile, your friend's late-night chats, or your kid's goofy dance. A 2024 UC Berkeley study found that people who regularly express gratitude report 25 percent higher life satisfaction. Appreciating others keeps you grounded in the now, reminding you that life's riches aren't just in achievements but also in relationships. When you thank your teammate for their hustle, you're not just building camaraderie—you're cultivating a mindset that finds joy in the everyday, making every step of your journey brighter.

Success, too, blooms from gratitude. People thrive in environments where they feel seen. When you catch your colleague acing a task and say, "You totally rocked that!" you're fostering a culture of growth. Research shows that workplaces with high appreciation see 30 percent more collaboration. Gratitude opens doors—your sincerity makes others want to work with you, share ideas, or cheer your wins. Plus, it's contagious. Your kind words inspire others to pay it forward, creating a cycle of upliftment that elevates everyone, including you.

How do you live this? Start small, with intention. Lean in and listen when someone shares their heart, whether it's your mom venting or a coworker brainstorming. Listening is love in action; it says, "You matter." Surprise someone with a heartfelt note or a coffee just because. These gestures, rooted in gratitude, forge bonds that anchor you through life's storms. Dr. Stephen G. Post's study at Stony Brook School of Medicine found that small acts of appreciation reduce stress by 20 percent, calming your mind for clearer, bolder decisions.

Gratitude for others also heals. In tough times, when loss or change clouds your view, thanking someone for their presence—like your friend who texts "You got this!"—reignites hope. It's not about ignoring pain but balancing it with love, reminding yourself you're not alone. This resilience is the backbone of a successful life, keeping you moving forward with grace.

So, dear one, make gratitude your daily ritual. Tell someone, "I'm so thankful for you." Compliment their spark, praise their effort, or just listen with a full heart. Each act is a step toward a life bursting with connection and purpose. You're not just appreciating others—you're crafting a masterpiece of joy and success, one kind moment at a time. Keep glowing, and know that your gratitude is changing the world, starting with your own happy heart.

What if you simply built a lovely life that makes you feel happy, that brings you joy, that is generative and supportive?"

—Jamie Varon, author, branding expert, and graphic designer

AFFIRMATION STATION

I don't wait for life to be perfect—
I thank it for what it is
and watch it become more.

Gratitude is my superpower.

When I focus on what's good,
the good multiplies.

I open my eyes to all that I already have.

CHAPTER 2

Creating a Manifestation Station

"What you radiate outward in your thoughts, feelings, mental pictures and words, you attract into your life."

—Catherine Ponder, American minister and founder of Unity Church Worldwide

I first heard the wisdom of the visionary teacher and writer Louise Hay twenty-five years ago. My dear friend Duncan gifted me his well-worn cassette tape of her speaking about how to develop a mindset of abundance. I admittedly brought a bit of a scarcity mindset to California with me from West Virginia and was eager to learn new ways. I loved Louise Hay's insights, which were wholly new to me. Duncan patiently explained to me his takeaways from Hay's wisdom and how it had worked for him to change his life for the better. When paying bills, instead of resenting the utility that supplies water and electricity, write the check, seal the envelope, and say aloud, "Thank you, Pacific Gas and Electric, for supplying me with power for my home and trusting me to pay you. Blessings to you, PG&E!" We began a ritual of paying bills together and then walking to the mailbox and pronouncing our gratitude to all the recipients of our money. We even added the finishing touch of kissing the stamped envelopes and saying, "Thank you!" before dropping them in for mailing. We got some looks of surprise at our mailbox rituals, but we believed wholeheartedly in Louise Hay, and doing that had been working for Duncan. Soon, it began to work for me, and I fully embraced the mindset. Most surprising of all, I stopped being filled with dread and worry when bills arrived and started paying them the same day they came in, whenever possible. In addition to adopting an attitude of abundance, it also helped my credit score!

In the early 1990s, we had to go to the mailbox for our five-minute gratitude ritual. Nowadays, with all the instantaneous ways of sending money and electronic payments, it might be closer to a five-second ritual. However, before you hit "Send," get into your Manifestor's Mindset and express thanks before you click or tap. This attitude of abundance that stems from the mindset is like a muscle; the more you use it, the stronger it will be, and you will see many manifestations.

A few years later, I met Louise Hay at INATS, the International New Age Trade Show in Denver, Colorado. It was a delightful event where people sold crystals, aura readings, candles, books, and every spiritual item you can possibly imagine. I still wear rings I got at INATS, some with shockingly large crystals and sacred stones that I treasure. When I walked into the concourse, I saw that Hay House had a booth, and Louise Hay herself was standing there, clad in light pink. My knees buckled. I knew I needed to thank her for all her wisdom that had truly changed my life. Back in the hotel room, I planned what I would say to her. The next morning, I went in a bit early to visit the Hay House booth. There she was, in luminous yellow. To me, Louise Hay was surrounded by a light; she seemed to glow. I nervously approached her and told her how her advice on paying bills had been transformational to me. She laughed and seemed tickled by my tale of West-Virginian-turned-Californian sticker shock. I thanked her profusely, and she insisted on gifting me more books she had written. She even signed them. By this point, I was very nearly exploding with gratitude. We hugged, and I floated away from her booth to my booth, riding high on such profoundly good vibes.

Louise Hay is no longer with us, but her brilliance and generosity of spirit remain. Thanks to all her books and audios, we can still learn from her.

Badass Manifesting: Crafting a Life You Love with Intention and Joy

Welcome to the art of badass manifesting—a vibrant, empowering approach to creating a life that hums with purpose, joy, and balance. This isn't about chasing hustle culture or forcing outcomes with gritted teeth. It's about aligning your heart, mind, and actions to invite what you truly desire, all while savoring the journey at a human pace. Think of it as planting seeds with love, tending them with care, and trusting the universe to help them bloom.

Manifesting starts with clarity. Picture your dream life—maybe it's a cozy home filled with laughter, a career that lights you up, or simply more time to sip herbal tea in your garden. Whatever it is, name it. Write it down, say it aloud, or pin it to a vision board. This act of declaring your desires is like setting a GPS for your soul. But don't stop there. Visualize it daily, feeling the warmth of that reality as if it's already yours. See yourself thriving, not just surviving.

A badass manifesting mindset thrives on positivity and resilience. Life can throw curveballs—burnout,

AFFIRMATION STATION

I am alive.

I have power.

It is real.

I now receive

the flow of plenty

with grace and gratitude.

self-doubt, or unexpected crises—but you're tougher than the toughest storms. Each morning, before the world rushes in, set an intention. It could be as simple as "I intend to feel calm and inspired today" or as bold as "I intend to attract opportunities that align with my purpose." Speak it, feel it, own it. This ritual grounds you, turning chaos into clarity and doubt into determination.

But manifesting isn't just wishful thinking—it's action with heart. Love cooking? Whip up a nourishing meal to fuel your body and soul. Crave peace? Try meditating or strolling through a park. These small, intentional acts weave wellness into your daily fabric, making space for YOU. They remind you that you're not just chasing goals; you're living them, one joyful moment at a time.

The magic of badass manifesting lies in trust. Let go of the need to control every detail. Instead, believe the universe is conspiring in your favor. Replace limiting beliefs like "I'm not enough" with affirmations like "I am worthy of abundance." Journal your dreams, celebrate your small wins, and practice gratitude for what's already yours. This energy shift opens doors you didn't even know existed.

Ultimately, badass manifesting is about crafting a life that feels like home—one filled with work you're proud of, relationships that uplift you, and moments that make your heart sing. It's not about perfection but progress, not about speed but savoring. So start today. Set your intention, take one bold step, and trust that you're cocreating something beautiful with the universe. Your dream life isn't just possible—it's already taking shape.

Visualize It! Intend It!

Wellness is a topic on nearly everyone's minds these days. We've learned that a life lived at breakneck speed comes to a screeching halt when we hit burnout or face a crisis. The purpose of this badass manifesting mindset is about making sure you never hit the wall and that your life is lived at a very human pace, filled with work you love and take pride in, and overflowing with joy. Your life needs to have room for YOU. Lots of it.

Thankfully, we humans are a resilient lot. By managing your time, you can enjoy cooking nutritious meals, meditating, and taking long walks in the park and neighborhood, healthy habits that many people have embraced. I highly recommend that you pry yourself away from the office to discover the true rapture of gardening, brewing herbal teas, cooking fresh homegrown veggies, and all the simple pleasures of a slower-paced lifestyle.

To embark upon lifelong well-being, you will need to bring this awareness to every day. Regular rituals go a long way to making visualization and intention a part of your daily life. Every single morning, before I even open

Ten Badass Manifesting Tips for a Joyful, Intentional Life

Ready to supercharge your manifesting game? These ten practical, upbeat tips will help you align your energy, actions, and intentions to create a life overflowing with joy and purpose.

- **SET A DAILY INTENTION:** Kick off each morning by stating a clear, positive intention. Example: "I intend to approach today with confidence and creativity." Say it aloud or write it down to set the tone.
- **VISUALIZE WITH FEELING:** Spend two to three minutes picturing your goal as if it's happening now. Feel the excitement, peace, or pride. The more vivid the emotion, the stronger the signal to the universe.
- **KEEP IT POSITIVE:** Frame intentions in a way that uplifts you. Instead of "I won't stress," try "I intend to feel calm and focused." Positive words amplify positive energy.
- **SIMPLIFY YOUR DESIRES:** Don't overwhelm yourself with a laundry list. Focus on one or two key goals, like "I intend to attract a fulfilling job" or "I intend to nurture my health."

- **ACT WITH PURPOSE:** Manifesting loves action. Want a new career? Update your résumé or network. Crave wellness? Cook a healthy meal or try yoga. Small steps bridge dreams to reality.
- **BUST LIMITING BELIEFS:** Notice thoughts like "I can't do this." Counter them with affirmations: "I am capable and deserving." Journaling helps uncover and shift these mental blocks.
- **CREATE A RITUAL:** Build manifesting into your routine. Try a vision board, morning affirmations, or the 3-6-9 Method (write your intention three times in the morning, six in the afternoon, nine at night).
- **TRUST THE PROCESS:** Let go of obsessing over "when" or "how." Trust that the universe is aligning things behind the scenes. Ascend to the top of the ridge, where the view is better.
- **CELEBRATE SMALL WINS:** Acknowledge every step forward, like a great interview or a peaceful day. Celebrating progress will fuel your motivation.

These tips are your tool kit for badass manifesting. Stay consistent, keep your heart open, and watch your intentions bloom into reality!

my eyes, I set an intention for my day. I visualize how the day will go and state my intention aloud for it to turn out well. I then state my vision for the day aloud. This practice takes only a few moments and sets a positive tone for my day. Because I set a daily intention, I begin each day calm, grounded, and centered. Your intentions and your ritual should be what works for YOU. Below is an example of a recent intention, which I hope can serve as encouragement for you. I intend this to work extremely well for you!

BADASS PRACTICE: DAILY MORNING INTENTION

Here's my intention: "I intend today's writing to flow easily, filled with inspiration that results in messages that help people and fill their hearts with happiness."

Now Set Your Own Intention!

1. State your intention. When you decide what you want, vocalize it or write it down.
2. Be clear.
3. Make sure your intention is positive.
4. Keep your intention simple.
5. Shift any limiting beliefs.

The Art of Visualization: Manifesting Your Badass Dreams with Gratitude

In my three decades in San Francisco, I've seen dreamers of every stripe—tech wizards, artists, activists, you name it—chasing their big, bold visions in this electric city. But here's the secret sauce I've learned: Visualization, that New Age superpower, isn't just about picturing your dream life. It's about feeling it, believing it, and wrapping it in gratitude to make it real. When you visualize with a thankful heart, you're not just manifesting—you're becoming the badass creator of your own destiny.

I first stumbled into visualization as a young woman, fresh out of college, working in publishing and navigating the wild world of authors and deadlines. I'd sit in my tiny Mission District apartment sipping coffee, staring at the fog rolling in, and imagine myself thriving, not just surviving, in my career. I'd close my eyes and see myself nailing presentations, laughing with colleagues, and signing my name in a book of my own someday. But the game changer? I'd whisper "Thank you" to the universe for every detail of that vision, as if it were already real. That gratitude anchored me, turning hazy dreams into vivid realities.

Visualization is like creating a mental movie where you're the star, director, and grateful audience all at once.

It's not about forcing outcomes or pretending you've got it all figured out. It's about painting a picture so clear—say, running your own business, finding love, or owning a sunlit loft in Noe Valley—that your heart says, "Yes, this is me." Then, you infuse it with thanks for what's already good in your life. That combo of clarity and gratitude? It's rocket fuel for manifestation.

My dad, the ultimate people person, taught me to connect with others, but visualization taught me to connect with myself. I'd picture calm conversations with tough clients, feeling grateful for my ability to listen, and suddenly, those calls went smoother. I'd visualize friendships that lit up my life, giving thanks for the ones I already had, and soon, new soulmates showed up. Gratitude keeps your vision grounded, reminding you that you're not starting from zero—you're building on a foundation of blessings.

Here's the deal: Visualization works because it rewires your brain to spot opportunities. When you're thankful for what you've got, you're not chasing from a place of lack. You're open, confident, and ready to receive. I'm grateful every day for the San Francisco hustle that showed me this—those steep hills taught me to keep climbing, and the vibrant people reminded me to dream big. Visualization isn't magic; it's a practice, a love letter to your future self, sealed with gratitude.

So grab a journal, a vision board, or just a quiet corner of your mind. Picture your badass life—maybe it's leading a team, traveling the world, or simply feeling at peace. Feel the joy of it, see the colors, hear the sounds. Then, say "Thank you" for the steps you've already taken, the strength you already have. You're not just visualizing—you're manifesting with a grateful heart; and that, my friend, is the most badass gratitude of all. Thank you, universe, for the dreams we get to chase and the gratitude that lights the way.

> "Ask once, believe you have received, and all you have to do to receive is feel good."
>
> *—Rhonda Byrne, Australian television writer and producer*

Mastering the Art of Visualization with Gratitude

- **CREATE A SACRED SPACE:** Find a cozy spot—your favorite café or a quiet corner at home. Light a candle, play soft music, and thank the universe for this moment to dream.
- **GET SPECIFIC:** Picture your goal vividly: leading a meeting, buying a home, or feeling confident. Note colors, sounds, and emotions. Gratitude for clarity makes it real.
- **FEEL THE FEELS:** Immerse yourself in the joy of your vision. Feel the pride, love, or peace. Say thanks for the emotions already in your life that match this vibe.
- **USE A VISION BOARD:** Collect images, quotes, or mementos that spark your dream. Place them where you'll see them daily, and thank your current blessings for inspiring you.
- **JOURNAL YOUR VISION:** Write your dream as if it's happening now. Start with "I'm so grateful for ..." to anchor it in thankfulness. Revisit and tweak weekly.

- **PRACTICE DAILY:** Spend five to ten minutes visualizing each morning or night. Consistency builds belief. Be thankful for the discipline you're cultivating.
- **PAIR WITH AFFIRMATIONS:** Say, "I'm grateful for my courage to manifest [my goal]." Positive words amplify your vision and gratitude.
- **RELEASE DOUBT:** When fear creeps in, acknowledge it, then let it go. Thank your journey for teaching you resilience, and refocus on your vision.
- **CELEBRATE SMALL WINS:** Notice steps toward your goal—a new connection, a bold move. Gratitude for progress fuels bigger manifestations.

- **STAY OPEN TO SURPRISES:** Your vision might evolve. Trust the process, and give thanks for the universe's creative twists.

Why Setting Intentions Works

Setting intentions is like programming your internal GPS. Your brain's reticular activating system (RAS) filters the chaos of the world based on what you focus on. When you set a clear intention—like "I'm going to radiate confidence today" or "I'm open to new opportunities"—you're telling your brain's RAS what to prioritize. Suddenly, you notice people, moments, and resources aligned with that vibe. It's not woo-woo; it's neuroscience with a side of soul. Intentions also anchor you emotionally. Life's a wild ride; and without a focal point, it's easy to get tossed around by stress, doubt, or other people's noise. An intention is your North Star, keeping you steady when the world tries to throw you off. It's not about forcing outcomes but about choosing how you show up. That's where the magic happens—because how you show up shapes what shows up for you.

On a deeper level, intentions tap into energy. Call it "quantum," "spiritual," or "the universe's vibe"—when you declare what you want with clarity and heart, you're putting out a signal. You're aligning your thoughts, emotions, and actions, which creates a ripple effect. Ever notice how people are drawn to you when you're in your power? That's intention at work, pulling in what matches your frequency.

How Setting Intentions Works

First, get clear. Vague intentions like "I want to be happy" are cute but useless. Dig deeper. What does happiness look like today? Maybe it's "I'm going to savor every conversation" or "I'll treat myself with kindness." Specificity is your superpower. Write it down, say it out loud, or meditate on it—whatever grounds you.

Next, feel it. Intentions aren't just words; they're a vibe. Close your eyes and imagine embodying that intention. Want to lead with courage? Picture yourself walking into a room, shoulders back, voice steady, owning your space. Let that feeling sink into your bones. Your emotions are the fuel that makes intentions stick.

Then, act like you mean it. Intentions aren't a set-it-and-forget-it deal. They're a commitment to align your actions with your vision. If you intend to cultivate peace, don't spend your day doomscrolling or picking fights. Make choices that match your goal—maybe it's a walk in nature or saying no to drama. Small, intentional steps compound into big shifts.

Timing matters too. Mornings are gold for setting intentions because your mind's fresh, but you can do it anytime—before a big meeting, a tough convo, or even midday when you need a reset. Rituals help; light a candle, sip your coffee mindfully, or jot your intention in a journal. Make it yours, something that feels like *you*.

Why This Matters for You, Badass

Here's the real tea: Setting intentions is about reclaiming your power. The world will try to tell you who you are or what you should want, but intentions let you write your own story. They remind you that you're not a passenger in your life—you're the driver. Whether you're chasing big dreams, healing from heartbreak, or just trying to survive a chaotic week, intentions give you agency. They're a gentle nudge to show up as the person you know you're meant to be—flawed, fierce, and unstoppable.

Start small, stay consistent, and trust the process. Set an intention today. Feel it, live it, own it. You've got this. And the universe? It's got your back.

Badass Inspiration: Face a Fear and Conquer It

I count myself as fortunate not to have many regrets. The ones I do have come from when I didn't try something. There was that one time I was too embarrassed to take up an instrument as an adult because I worried about how terrible I would sound; there was also one instance when I didn't try a sport or join a group activity because I felt awkward. In hindsight, that all seems so silly to me. No one was judging me except myself!

Let go of all that baggage and try new things. Learn as you go, and you will learn as you grow! I call this "Imagine a Day," where you try something new and just do it!

Here is what I now know to be true: A lack of imagination is the only limitation, and fear creates self-doubt. Take yourself out of fear mode and unlock the power of your imagination. I urge you to Imagine a Day: Pick something you've always wanted to do but have been afraid to try. Painting, French cookery, playing piano, singing, learning a foreign language, yoga, rock-climbing, ballroom dancing, pottery, snorkeling—something that speaks to you on a profound level but scares you a little. Find a class, or barter with someone who is an expert whom *you* can teach something, and dive right in. Live your life no holds barred and regret-free!

BADASS PRACTICE: YOUR GOALS WILL GROW YOU

Make a list of short-term goals you would like to achieve by the end of the year, month, or even week. As you accomplish your goals, express gratitude for the effort, inspiration, people, and other factors that helped you along the way. My goal is to give more to those around me, near and far. I would love to hear your inspirations!

Badass Brilliance: Meditation Makes You Smarter (and Way Calmer)!

Did you know that having a regular mindfulness practice is not just good for your soul and your body but is also FANTASTIC for your brain? It is! Meditation creates new neural pathways, which keep you sharp, can prevent issues later in life, and help you fend off depression and boost your self-esteem. John Hopkins has conducted some very impressive studies on this.

Meditation doesn't have to be boring, and it doesn't always need to be done sitting in a lotus position on the floor. It can be very active and can include movement.

Try getting out of your head and into your heart.

Because the world we exist in today is very much about staying in your head, many of us must make a concentrated effort to become grounded and in touch with our bodies and the natural world. "Grounding" is a technique for centering yourself within your being. When you see someone driving past you talking on their cell phone, you know that they are not grounded—holding a phone and driving shows they are not *being here now*.

For deep grounding, try creative visualization or, better yet, a group or guided meditation.

"You are the creator of your own reality."

—Esther Hicks, American motivational speaker, channeler, and author

BADASS PRACTICE:
A WALKING MEDITATION WITH BENEFITS

This is the simplest of rituals, one you can do every day of your life. Go for a walk and, as you stroll, take the time to look and really see what is in your path. For example, my friend Eileen takes a bag with her and picks up pieces of what she calls "future recycling" (what most of us would call garbage) in her path. She does this as an act of love for the earth. During the ten years she's practiced this walking meditation, she has probably turned a mountain of potential garbage into upcycled and repurposed objects. Eileen is very grounded. She is also a deeply happy person who shares joy with all on her path.

Unplug and Recharge Your Battery

So many of us are tethered to our devices: smartphones, tablets, and even wearable monitors (like a Fitbit or smartwatch) that track every moment of our lives. They remind us about meetings, appointments, and other "emergencies" with chimes and all manner of alarms. We all have so much going on! Maybe too much. Here is a very simple and highly effective badass habit: Unplug!

Pick a day to not use any technological devices. Texting, checking your social media feed, watching your favorite YouTube channel, checking your email—all of them can wait until tomorrow! Turn off your devices and turn on your senses! Read a book, cook a meal, and enjoy the outdoors by taking a walk or tending to your garden. Technology distracts us from the real world, occupying our attention with games, chat rooms, social media, commercials, and so on. Want to know what's going on in the news? Read a newspaper. Be aware of the here and now by finding activities that don't require electricity or a battery. Make your own entertainment.

Acts of Kindness (Be Kind to Yourself Too)

I am very blessed to have been part of the team that brought the *Random Acts of Kindness* book to the world. It was a highlight of my career and imprinted on me the power of the human heart. Acts of kindness and adopting a kindness mindset is a wonderful thing to incorporate into your life.

Get acquainted with simple human kindness and easy acts of goodness every day. When at the grocery store, return the shopping cart or help the elderly person struggling with their bags. Open doors for people. Say "Hello" with a smile. Every day, and in every way, choose to take the high road in your travels.

Commit to refraining from negative self-talk. Be kind to yourself. The extremely wise Dawna Markova, the author of a favorite book, *I Will Not Die an Unlived Life*, says, "Your soul remembers when you put yourself down; it imprints upon you. Never do this. Self-compassion is key to a life well-lived."

Instant Kindness: Look Up!

Put down your smartphone and make eye contact, person to person. Nowadays, I consider that a major act of kindness and courtesy.

Badass Practice: DIY Optimism

Try this easy way to craft some kindness. Make a sign that reads "Take what you need," with tear-off tabs on the bottom that say "love," "courage," "optimism," and so on. Hang it up in places you regularly pass by. Keep refills at the ready!

How to Create a Manifestation Station

A Manifestation Station is your little corner of magic—a sacred spot in your home where gratitude and dreams come together to spark something amazing. It's a physical space, like a cozy desk nook or a small shelf, where you can focus on what you're thankful for and what you're calling into your life. I started mine a few years ago during a tough winter. I was feeling lost, so I cleared a corner of my bedroom desk, lit a tiny candle, and placed a photo of my family there. I'd sit with my morning coffee, say, "I'm grateful for these people," and write down one dream, like finding a job I loved. That space became my sanctuary, and within months, I landed an ideal situation.

Your Manifestation Station doesn't need to be fancy—it just needs to feel like YOU. Here's how to create one with love and intention.

Step 1: Pick Your Spot

Find a small space in your home that feels safe and comforting. It could be a corner of your desk, a windowsill, or a shelf. Make sure it's somewhere you can sit for a few minutes each day without distractions.

Step 2: Make It Yours

Add a few meaningful items. Maybe add a candle that smells comforting, a photo of someone you love, or a little plant that brings you joy. I keep a smooth stone I found on a beach—it reminds me of calm days. Choose things that make your heart smile.

Step 3: Add Gratitude and Dreams

Place a notebook or a stack of sticky notes at your station. Each day, write down one thing you're grateful for and one thing you're manifesting. For example, write "I'm grateful for my warm bed. I'm calling in a new friend who gets me." Keep these notes in a little jar or pin them up.

Step 4: Make It a Ritual

Spend a few minutes at your station daily. Light your candle, take a deep breath, and read your gratitude note out loud. Then, speak your dream, like you're inviting it in. Feel the gratitude in your bones—it's the fuel for your manifestations.

Step 5: Share the Magic

Invite a loved one to create their own Manifestation Station. Swap stories about your spaces and dreams over coffee or a call. You'll feel the warmth of building this practice together, knowing you're both rooting for each other.

Your Manifestation Station is your daily reminder that gratitude and dreams are a powerful duo. It's a space to hold your hopes, wrapped in thankfulness.

Badasses Can Change the World

In the hurly-burly of this busy world, simple kindness and goodness can get left behind in the rush to be first in line, to reach the top of the corporate ladder, and to have the most "likes." But what does it all mean at the end of the day? Aren't being a good person and making real contributions to the world more important than anything else?

In recent years, I have reflected on my childhood in the sylvan hills of West Virginia, where I was raised on a farm to follow the Golden Rule. When I first arrived in San Francisco—literally wearing a blue gingham dress—I could not get over the sophistication and urbanity of Northern California. I loved it but was *very* intimidated by the houses without front yards, the hair, the far-out fashions, the very mannered-ness of it all. I arrived with $500 in my pocket, thinking I could live on that for some months in San Francisco. (You can stop laughing now.) Once reality set in, I realized I needed to make money just to keep a roof over my head from one month to the next. This set me on a path of worrying about the bottom line as I worked two jobs and did my best to keep the coffers somewhat filled. I did notice over time, though, that I was not the same happy-go-lucky gingham gal that had rolled in from the sticks in the mid-eighties.

Over years of working for multinational corporations, I became a workaholic and worrywart. I had seized upon the goal to go global with my work. After much jockeying, many long hours, and doing whatever it took, I finally landed a job as a buyer for one of the world's largest import/export outfits. My duties would entail traveling the world and shopping—on somebody else's dime, mind you. I was thrilled and could not stop bragging to anyone that would listen about my new gig.

The big day arrived, and I was ushered into the office of the top boss to go over our itinerary, which included stops in India, China, Portugal, and Italy. When I was shown photos of the factories in China and India, I nearly fainted but blurted out, "Those are children. Our products are being made by children? How can this be?" I distinctly remember having an out-of-body experience. I was horrified to hear my own voice shrilly continuing, "All the products in India have to be spray lacquered. Where are the fans, and vents, and masks?" Suddenly, I realized my "dream job" was, in fact, a nightmare.

My boss, a former merchant marine who was tougher than any nail, coolly responded, "They feel they are lucky to have a job, and so should you."

I could not help myself from responding, "These kids will be coughing up their lungs before they're ten years old. This just isn't right. No way am I exploiting children, and neither should you."

I could hardly believe what was coming out of my mouth. Looking back, it is one of my proudest moments. This was when I was reminded of what really matters. I learned that the good teachings instilled in me by my family had taken root, even in this citified soil. From then on, I have become more conscious, day by day, of living a life based on values. I quit my job the next day, despite being scared to death of not having any income. I used my newfound skill to talk my way into a job in publishing, and best of all, with a publishing house specializing in philosophy, spirituality, self-help, and the wisdom traditions of the world. It even had a tree-planting program to offset its environmental impact.

At the end of one's life, I feel sure that having lots of money, fancy cars, and real estate will not be nearly as important as how much love one gave to the world.

Badass women don't just dream of a better world—they build it, one fearless leap at a time. My story is a testament to how a single moment of courage can spark a lifetime of impact, and it's a call to every woman to embrace her inner badass and change the world.

You, too, have that spark. Every woman does. Being a badass isn't about being fearless; it's about acting despite fear. It's daring to say no to what's wrong and yes to what's right, even when the path is uncertain. Maybe it's leaving a toxic job, starting a business that lifts others up, or speaking out against injustice in your community. Each leap, no matter how small, sends ripples of change. The world needs your courage. It needs you to trust your gut, to risk failure for what matters, to build a legacy of love and impact. You don't need a cape or a corner office—just the audacity to act. My stand against exploitation was a single step, but it taught me that badass women don't wait for permission. We create, we challenge, we transform.

So take the leap. Dare to be the woman who says, "This isn't right" and then makes it right. Your courage, your heart, your badass spirit—they're what will save the world, one bold move at a time.

Thank-You Notes to Those Who Helped You Along the Way

I am overflowing with badass gratitude for my parents, aunts, and teachers who forged my moral compass and gave me the spine to stand tall. Growing up in West Virginia's hills, they taught me the Golden Rule: Treat others with fairness and love. When I faced the soul-crushing reality of my new job, one that entailed exploiting children, their lessons roared to life. Quitting wasn't just a choice—it was an uprising against wrong, fueled by the values they instilled. Their wisdom gave me the guts to walk away, trusting my heart over fear. To every woman reading this: Honor those who shaped your courage. Their teachings are your power to change the world, one badass step at a time.

Badass gratitude isn't just feeling thankful—it's expressing it boldly! To honor those who instilled your values, try these four tips:

1. **Write a heartfelt letter:** Share a specific memory of how their guidance, like my parents' Golden Rule, shaped your courage to stand for what's right.
2. **Call or visit:** Tell them directly how their wisdom empowered you, as my teachers empowered me to quit an exploitative job.
3. **Pay it forward:** Mentor someone else, passing on the values your aunt taught you.
4. **Post a public tribute:** Share their impact on you on social media to inspire others. Expressing gratitude amplifies your mentors' legacy and fuels your badass mission to change the world, one thank-you at a time.

AFFIRMATION STATION

My spirit is peaceful, intentional, and full of purpose.

I create sacred ground within myself.

The energy I nurture echoes into my life.

I am the architect of my joy.

CHAPTER 3

The Importance of Aligning Yourself with Other Grateful Badasses

"Friends. Sisters. Mothers. Professors. When women affirm women, it unlocks our power. It gives us permission to shine brighter."

—Elaine Welteroth, American journalist, editor, author, and television host

I am eternally grateful that I learned from my dad how to talk to anyone, anytime. My mother is the exact opposite, very shy and timid. When I was really little, I was my dad's buddy and would accompany him in the farm truck to pick up supplies, anything from feed for the animals in winter to extensive explorations of the hardware store for a seemingly endless renovation of the barn. He knew everyone's name, and they always seemed happy to see him. Soon, I was greeted like he was, probably a source of amusement: My mom dressed me for these outings in frilly church dresses.

I was a very sober youngster, not easily given to smiles. My best guess is that I was simply trying to figure everything out, and the outside world seemed mighty strange to my child's mind.

But there was always a lot of joshing and merriment at the feed store, hardware store, and plant nursery when Dad and I rolled up. He was just easy to talk to! And it didn't take long for me to loosen up and smile along with everyone else, especially when I got a delectable piece of candy or bubble gum. Even at gas stations and garages where Dad didn't know a soul, he would offer a friendly "Hey, neighbor!" That simple icebreaker always did the trick, and the next time, they would greet him by name and eventually become part of the entourage. I kid you not—he had more friends than anyone else I have ever known. By third grade, I had developed a variation of my dad's people skills. By the time I was in high school, Mom complained that I had too many friend activities, too many people stopping by, slews of sleepovers, and that my girl gaggle and I needed to be driven hither and thither. When she said, "You're just like your dad," which she meant as an invective, I felt like I had hit the jackpot!

When I started working after college, one of my first jobs was in customer service, which I really liked and for which I seemed to have a natural talent. Somehow, I was often able to calm the savage beast, soothe upset customers, and make them feel like they had an ally. Coworkers started to ask if I could handle the really difficult customers, the most upset and angry folks. I was happy to do that, and eventually, it was a company practice to "transfer the crazy callers to Becca." To be honest, I didn't have any special skills, but I tried to emulate my dad by talking to anyone at any time. When I got my first job in publishing, the same thing happened with authors, who mostly just wanted a listening ear. There, I earned the moniker The Author Whisperer. I marvel that I learned all this at feed stores.

Thank you, Dad, for teaching me how to talk to anyone, anytime, anywhere. It is an incredible life skill. Much more important, it has brought enormous joy into my life. I have many lifelong friendships, some of which started when in third grade.

My dad was a total and completely badass in the art of friendship. You, too, can be a badass friend. To be honest, it is pretty easy and worth every minute of effort.

Don't Go It Alone

Being creative or an artist can be very lonely, but it doesn't have to be. Most people reach the height of their talent by exchanging ideas and inspiration with others. The art of friendship, which is highly creative, is even more so when practiced in a supportive circle.

Invite a group of like-minded people over to participate in a creative activity. Begin by opening your space and dedicating the time to this enterprise. Go around the group and talk about your goals and what you need. Within minutes, group members will offer help to each other. See? No need to go it alone!

The Art of Friendship: Badass Gratitude in Action

Badasses don't just build friendships; we craft lifelines. Our bonds are forged in laughter, tea-soaked afternoons, and moments that remind us to stay grateful for the people who hold us up. Friendship, for us, is an art—a practice of showing up with heart, grit, and badass gratitude that transforms lives.

My friends and I gather regularly; sometimes Zoom will have to do, but our bonds are sacred. We share stories and sweets, but the real magic happens when we let our masks drop. One night, after I gave away the expensive cookies from that store *How a Place of Cookies*

Can Change a Life to a young mother in need, my friends didn't bat an eye at the empty table. Instead, they leaned in. We talked about luck, love, and how to lift others up. That's friendship: seeing the bigger picture, choosing connection over perfection.

Badass gratitude means celebrating your tribe fiercely hyping their wins, holding their hands through storms. It's texting "You've got this" at two in the morning or listening without fixing. It's knowing that a single moment—a shared laugh, a quiet nod—can change someone's day. Gratitude fuels us to show up, not just for each other but for the world, like passing along a paper bag of hope to a stranger.

This art isn't about grand gestures. It's the small, brave acts: forgiving a friend's flaws, owning your own, and saying "Thank you" for the people who make you better. Badasses build friendships that ripple outward, reminding us we're never alone. So gather your crew, share your stories, and let gratitude lead. Because with your supporters by your side, every moment is a chance to change a life—maybe even yours!

Authentically Is Everything

- **SHOW UP AUTHENTICALLY:** Drop the masks and share your real self—flaws, dreams, and all. True friendship thrives on vulnerability and honesty.
- **PRACTICE BADASS GRATITUDE:** Celebrate your friends' wins, and thank them for their presence. Gratitude turns good moments into lasting bonds.
- **LEAN INTO SMALL MOMENTS:** A quick text, a shared laugh, or a quiet listen can be as powerful as grand gestures to build deep connections.
- **SUPPORT WITHOUT FIXING:** Be there for your friends' struggles with empathy, not solutions, unless they ask. Your presence is often enough.
- **GIVE BACK TOGETHER:** Like passing cookies to a stranger, let your friendships inspire acts of kindness that ripple into the world.
- **FORGIVE AND GROW:** Embrace your friends' imperfections and your own. Strong friendships are built on grace and mutual growth.

"Don't let anyone else take away your joy. If they don't want to be with you or around you, let them go."

—Gabourey Sidibe, American actress

Fast Friends: A Badass Gal Pal Group Affirmation

I firmly believe that our friends are some of the greatest loves of our lives. When you instantly click with another badass woman, she may well be worth cultivating as a pal. Some of the most memorable times of my life have been high-quality time with my girlfriends. We regularly have gal-pal gatherings, and I recommend you do the same. Here is one that is pure fun and a very good time!

Get a bunch of inexpensive pins at a dime store; I get mine at Dollar Tree. They are very cute and easy on the pocketbook, with hearts, flowers, trees, stones, coins, cats, puppies, moons, stars, suns, and myriad bright and happy images. Pin these charms onto your gal pals' garments, ideally over the heart. They should represent the good fortune you wish for your friend: coins for money, a heart shape for love, a sun for luck and happiness, a pyramid or moon for wisdom, or whatever suits you. Others can pick out pins for you, as everyone should participate in the fun and mutual acknowledgment. Feel free to use your imagination, and remember to use this only for positive associations.

Say aloud this group affirmation:

To ____, I give all the luck in the world.

To ____, I give all the money in the world.

To ____, I give all the wisdom of the sages.

To ____, I give all the joy of love.

With love and joy to all that we shall enjoy together!

Emotional Intelligence: Transforming Every Facet of Life

I'm endlessly thankful for the gift of connecting with people, a skill I picked up watching my dad charm everyone he met. Emotional intelligence (EI)—the ability to understand and manage your emotions while tuning in to others'—is a life-changer. To develop it, start by truly listening, catching the nuances in someone's tone or expression, and responding with care. Self-awareness is key; recognize when you're upset or withdrawn, like I was as a serious kid trying to make sense of the world. Reflect on your feelings, and choose how to act rather

AFFIRMATION STATION

I count my blessings.

I choose to focus on the good things.

I vow to give back when I can.

than react. Empathy is the heart of it—imagine yourself in another's place: whether they're a frustrated colleague or a close friend. This skill grows with practice, like my dad's warm greetings that turned strangers into friends. Emotional intelligence enhances every part of your life. It strengthens relationships, defuses workplace tension, and makes you a steady presence for loved ones. You'll navigate conflicts calmly, advance your career through better connections, and find inner peace. It's not just a tool—it's a way to live more fully, forging deeper bonds and approaching challenges with clarity. Like my dad's effortless way with people, emotional intelligence brings joy and ease to your days, making every interaction richer and every moment brighter.

> "It is a blessing to know a free woman. Sometimes she will stop by and hold up a mirror for you. She will help you remember who you are."
>
> —*Glennon Doyle, author and activist*

BADASS PRACTICE: MESSAGE IN A BOTTLE

If you and a friend have argued and you want to heal the wound, try this simple ritual. It is remarkably effective and can even be used for bigger issues. If you have a letter or even a printed email from your friend discussing the conflict, roll it into a scroll, place it in a green glass bottle, and cork the bottle. If you don't have such a document, write one. One evening, when it is still light outside, take the bottle to a river or ocean at low tide. Draw a heart on the outside of the bottle with a permanent marker, then toss it gently into the water so it doesn't break.

Wait until the bottle has disappeared and concentrate on your desire to make up with your friend. Wait a full twenty-four hours before contacting your friend. With the rising tide the following day, the waters of peace between you will also rise.

Badass Emotional Intelligence

- **LISTEN LIKE A BADASS:** Tune in fully, no distractions, catching every word and vibe. It's a gratitude-fueled superpower that makes people feel seen, cementing you as their go-to confidant.
- **OWN YOUR EMOTIONS WITH GRIT:** Spot when you're upset or down, and name it. This badass self-awareness keeps you steady, letting you tackle life's chaos with unshakable calm.
- **EMPATHIZE LIKE A CHAMPION:** Dive into others' feelings, whether they're raging or rejoicing. This EI edge turns fleeting chats into deep bonds, and you'll be very thankful for the connections it sparks.
- **RESPOND WITH BADASS GRACE:** Keep your cool with even the toughest folks. A thoughtful word shuts down drama, earning you respect and gratitude for staying true to your values.

- **REFLECT LIKE A PRO:** After a heated exchange, replay it and learn from it. This badass habit sharpens your EI, turning every misstep into a chance to grow stronger and wiser.

- **SPREAD JOY LIKE A ROCK STAR:** Share positivity, like a bold compliment or a warm nod. It's a gratitude-driven act that forges epic friendships and makes your life a celebration.

Why go all in? Because badass emotional intelligence makes you a force—unstoppable in relationships, unstoppable at work, unstoppable in life. It's easy to kick off, and the payoff is massive: richer connections, skyrocketing confidence, and a heart full of gratitude for the vibrant life you're building. Be a badass, embrace EI, and watch your world light up.

Knitting the Bonds of Female Friendship

From time immemorial, women have been very crafty. Healers from ancient times were extremely resourceful because they had to be; they needed to take care of their families and, oftentimes, their community. They mastered the art of growing and foraging for the bounty of the fields and forests, searching for herbs and roots for medicine and food to feed the tribe. This same resourcefulness gave our elders an advantage with crafting, as they were thrifty, and good at figuring out how to repurpose and get the most possible use out of whatever they had. Those same traits and talents have been passed down to us; crafty women are everywhere today, and you can often find their wares at metaphysical bookstores, apothecaries, and so many other retailers, including Etsy. When I was a little girl growing up on a farm, my aunts seemingly knew every craft—they were such gifted and creative women! Aunt Ida made doilies that the Etsy crowd would covet, while her sister, Ivy, tatted the most perfect lace; it was stunningly beautiful.

I was taught how to sew, quilt, and crochet by my mother, Helen, and her sister, Aunt Ruth, who was a fantastic cook and gardener. As soon as I could toddle behind her in the garden, I learned how to plant flowers and veggies, and I was quite proud of myself that I knew how to propagate and graft plants. If you ever take a drive with me in the countryside, be prepared to stop often so we can get clippings for starters from what's growing on the side of the road (don't worry, we will be careful to pull as far off as possible, and you'll be quite safe). I do this so often, I even keep a kit in the trunk of my old hybrid for this purpose. I have a few prized fruit trees that didn't cost a penny, coming from the bounty of Mother Earth.

My mom's best friend, Marilyn, had a loom in her living room that she and her mother, who had the unforgettable and charming name Dixie, used daily. This clever duo ripped any old towels, socks, garments, and even tea towels judged to be past their prime into small pieces and turned them into rag rugs. While the name is humble and homely, the rugs Dixie and Marilyn crafted were not. They were wonderfully colorful, felt good under your toes, and brightened any room. We brought worn-out fabric over to their house and feasted on tea cakes while they produced the rugs, even during our visit. Their production crafting became so popular that they started selling them from their home at a fast clip. I have one of Marilyn and Dixie's eye-catching works of art at my kitchen sink. Every time I see it, I think of how they gathered in friendship and, through their pure ingenuity, spun old rags into gold.

I was lucky indeed to grow up on a farm surrounded by crafty relatives and friends. My aunties and mom and her dearest friends were unforgettably badass crafters; and they had also mastered the art of loving friendship, seeing each other through illnesses, divorce, money woes, and bereavement. These women were strong to begin with, but together, they were forces of nature. Even if you, like me, have all thumbs on each hand, join a gaggle of crafty women. Go for the tea cozy projects; and stay for the comforting love and unstinting support.

Badass Crafting Circles: Weaving Friendship with Creativity

Since ancient times, women have been the ultimate creators, stitching together not just fabric but the very bonds of community. Healers and homemakers, they've foraged herbs, grown food, and turned scraps into treasures with fierce ingenuity.

A crafting circle is more than a hobby group—it's a sisterhood forged in creativity. Whether you're crocheting like my mother, Helen, taught me, grafting fruit trees from roadside clippings, or dreaming up something new, the act of making together builds trust and vulnerability. You share your flaws, your dreams, and your half-finished projects, laughing over dropped stitches or celebrating a perfect seam. These circles echo the resourcefulness of our ancestors, who knew how to make do and make magic. They're a rebellion against throwaway culture, a reminder that we can transform scraps—literal and emotional—into art.

When women craft together, they weave something deeper than thread. They create space for authenticity, where a quiet listen or a shared triumph strengthens bonds. Like Marilyn and Dixie, whose rag rugs became a neighborhood sensation, a crafting circle can spark joy that ripples outward. It's a place to honor the women who came before us, to channel their thrifty brilliance, and to build friendships that feel like family. So gather your girls, grab your tools, and start crafting. In the clatter of creativity, you'll find the heartbeat of connection—strong, vibrant, and beautifully badass.

> "Don't forget: hold somebody's hand through the dark."
>
> *—Joy Harjo, Mvskoke poet, musician, playwright, and author*

How to Set Up and Maintain a Badass Crafting Circle

- **CURATE YOUR CREW WITH INTENTION:** Invite women who spark joy and share your love for creating—friends, neighbors, or new faces. Keep the group small (six to ten people) for intimacy, ensuring everyone feels seen. Choose a mix of skill levels to inspire learning and collaboration.

- **SET A SACRED SPACE:** Pick a cozy, well-lit spot—a living room, backyard, or community center. Clear tables for supplies, add comfy seating, and set the vibe with candles or music. Make it a haven where creativity and connection flow freely.

- **DEFINE THE VIBE, NOT THE CRAFT:** Let everyone bring their passion—knitting, sewing, macramé, or even potion-making. Avoid rigid rules; the goal is freedom to create. Rotate who suggests the next project to keep things fresh and inclusive.

- **SCHEDULE WITH CONSISTENCY:** Commit to a regular rhythm—weekly, bimonthly, or monthly—to build momentum. Use a group chat or calendar invites to stay organized. Respect everyone's time by starting and ending promptly, leaving room for lingering chats over snacks.

- **FOSTER CONNECTION BEYOND CRAFTS:** Encourage vulnerability and gratitude. Start sessions with a quick check-in: Share a win, a struggle, or a funny story. Celebrate finished projects with cheers, and honor the process with empathy. Bring snacks to share to fuel the soul.

- **KEEP THE CIRCLE THRIVING:** Maintain the group's energy by welcoming new ideas and members sparingly to preserve the vibe. Organize occasional group projects, like making gifts for a local shelter, to channel your collective badassery. If conflicts arise, address them with grace, prioritizing open communication to protect the sisterhood.

A crafting circle is a living thing, nurtured by authenticity and care. It's not just about what you make but who you become together. With these tips, you'll create a space where friendships deepen, creativity soars, and every stitch strengthens the bonds that hold you tight.

Breakups Hurt, Especially Friend Breakups

Releasing a toxic friendship is a gut-wrenching yet liberating act of self-love, especially when loyalty keeps you tethered to someone who's become a frenemy. I learned this the hard way with a dear friend whose undiagnosed mental illness turned our bond into a battlefield. She was once a vibrant part of our tight-knit friend group, but her untreated struggles morphed her into someone who lashed out, sowing discord until she'd alienated everyone. I clung to the friendship out of loyalty, hoping the "old her" would return, but it drained me. Watching her spiral while pushing us away was heartbreaking, yet I had to let go to protect my peace. If you're facing a similar struggle, here's how to release a toxic friendship with badass gratitude and gentle strength.

First, face the truth head-on. My friend's erratic behavior—snide remarks, unpredictable outbursts— wasn't just "her being her"; it was toxic. Accepting that her mental health struggles didn't excuse the harm gave me clarity.

Reflect on moments that hurt you to affirm your choice. Next, set boundaries with compassion. I didn't confront her harshly; instead, I stepped back, limiting contact with a kind but firm message: "I care, but this isn't working for me." You're not abandoning them—you're honoring yourself.

Then, grieve the loss. I journaled about our good times, cried for what was, and forgave myself for not fixing her. Therapy helped me process the guilt of moving on while she struggled.

Finally, pour that energy back into you. I reconnected with our friend group, picked up painting, and rediscovered joy in my own company. Letting go isn't betrayal; it's a bold reclaiming of your light.

You're not alone in this. Releasing my friend was painful, but it freed me to nurture relationships that lift me instead. You deserve that too—embrace the strength to choose yourself with grace and grit.

- *Face the Truth*: Identify specific toxic behaviors to validate your decision to step away.
- *Set Boundaries with Compassion*: Communicate your needs clearly, prioritizing your well-being.
- *Grieve the Loss*: Process emotions through journaling or therapy to release guilt.
- *Reinvest in Yourself*: Rediscover joy in hobbies and healthy connections.

A Plate of Cookies Can Change a Life

You know how certain memories sometimes remain crystal clear, as though they are trapped in the amber of your consciousness? While I don't know nearly enough about how the brain works, I suspect these shards of memory that stay with us are some of the most important events of our lives, to be pondered for all they contain. They might be teachable moments for us to draw upon. While the neuroscience aspects elude me, I do know the following memory is a life lesson.

My besties and I like to have a cup of tea now and again, the fancy kind with tea cakes, cupcakes, and cookies that are almost too beautiful to eat. During my decade in the Lower Haight, my dear friends and I got together once a month, taking turns at each other's houses. I was excited to be hosting one lovely spring day and planned everything, from the tea cakes and lemon cakes with lime icing, mini cupcakes with lacy designs, and my favorite black-and-white cookies, chocolate on one side, vanilla on the other. I even had brightly colored paper napkins with fiery wild-woman quotes on them.

I was working in Berkeley and living in San Francisco, which meant that just getting home across the Bay Bridge was going to be an adventure. On this day, it would be a miracle. I was terrified my friends would be waiting for me at the front door while I navigated the traffic. I surrendered to it, knowing my anxiety would not change a thing. Plus, I had my secret weapon: the nicest array of confections ever. How could they be mad at me when I was bringing them stunningly beautiful cookies on napkins that reminded them they're fabulous?

Finally, my lane of traffic oozed off the Fremont exit into downtown San Francisco. I was going to bust out one of my special moves and drive down a one-way artery to avoid the clogged streets. To do that, I had to drive past the Transbay Terminal, one of the most desolate and derelict spots in the entire greater Bay Area. I was chugging along and feeling good about my bag of goodies when I was slowed again by a Muni bus lumbering along at what appeared to be three miles per hour. But I still had my special treats, and my confidence remained intact.

I looked to my left, and a mother and her toddler were standing on the raised median about two feet away from my car. She looked not much older than a teenager and had a frightened look and a big bruise on her cheek. Her little boy was hugging her knee, trying to stay warm in the arctic wind that blasts San Francisco as soon as the sun sets. I smiled at them, and she smiled back, which is when I saw she was missing at least one tooth. In this moment, I just knew she had run away from an abusive home and was getting herself and her son to safety. I also knew in that moment that they needed money. I scrambled around in my messy purse but could only find a five-dollar bill, as I had spent all my cash on the sweets. I grabbed the pretty paper bag filled with boxes of delicacies and shoved it into her hands along with the wadded-up bill. The look on her face will stay with me for a lifetime. She was surprised, and the stress drained out of her face so I could see how pretty she was. The bus shot forward, and I had to drive away, but I managed to shout back at her, "These are the best cookies in the world, so everything is going to be okay!" I looked in the rearview mirror and saw her bend down. She opened a box and lovingly fed her little boy one of my treasured black-and-whites. They were laughing, and her son was even dancing around. My heart lifted as I drove away. I was especially pleased that the sassy paper napkins were going to remind this young woman of her fabulousness.

My girlfriends and I microwaved popcorn that night, but nobody minded. We also ended up having a much deeper and richer discussion about real things—no shopping talk, no boyfriend problems. We talked about how lucky we were and ways we could give back to the world.

It's funny how I knew those cookies were going to save the night. I guess I just didn't know whose.

AFFIRMATION STATION

I attract the right people
by speaking my truth.

Alignment isn't luck—it's a decision
I make every day to live with purpose.

I honor myself by surrounding myself
with those who honor me too.

I receive the love I give.

CHAPTER 4

How to Turn a Baditude into an Attitude of Gratitude

"You have been criticizing yourself for years, and it hasn't worked. Try approving of yourself and see what happens."

—Louise L. Hay, American motivational author, professional speaker, and AIDS activist

Let's face it: We live in a stressed-out world. Just watching the evening news may make you want to hide under the covers or disengage altogether. Many of my friends have gone on a very strict news "diet" and are surprised when I mention a major media story. Others in my circle do a lot of doomscrolling and are racked with worry as a result. I get it, and I completely understand both of those instincts. As I write this, there are predictions that shelves will be empty by the holiday and that parents won't be able to afford toys for their children. (May I recommend children's books as a worthy substitute?) It can look bleak and leave us feeling beleaguered. Just shopping for groceries and filling the gas tank of my hybrid can be traumatizing. But you can't let those external forces control your daily life. You must be the captain of your own ship and navigate through the rapids and uncertainties of the world around you.

It all starts with your mindset. Mindset really is everything.

How to Develop a Badass Positive Mindset

You must own your own inner strength and exude positivity, centered in the peaceful sense of gratitude you have for the blessings in your life. No matter what life throws at you, hold on to that strong, peaceful center. It is more than just thinking happy thoughts. It is about your rock-solid sense of self as a badass with unshakable confidence and the resilience that will get you through anything. This mindset can be the rudder by which you steer your proverbial ship. You can absolutely be the master of your own fate and have a joy-filled, successful, and happily badass life.

Embracing a positive badass mindset is about cultivating unshakable confidence, resilience, and a fearless approach to life's challenges. It's not just about being tough—it's about blending optimism with grit, turning setbacks into comebacks, and owning your unique strengths. This mindset empowers you to chase your goals relentlessly, radiate positivity, and inspire others along the way. It requires intentional effort, self-awareness, and a commitment to growth. By shifting your perspective, mastering your emotions, and taking bold action, you can transform how you navigate the world. A positive badass mindset isn't about ignoring reality; it's about facing it head-on with courage and the belief that you can handle anything. Ready to unleash your inner powerhouse? Here's how to build a mindset that's equal parts bold, positive, and unstoppable:

- *Practice Self-Affirmation Daily:* Reinforce your worth with positive, empowering statements to build confidence.
- *Embrace Challenges as Growth:* View obstacles as opportunities to learn and strengthen your resilience.
- *Surround Yourself with Positivity:* Seek supportive, uplifting people who fuel your drive and optimism.
- *Set Bold, Clear Goals:* Define ambitious objectives to channel your energy and maintain focus.

- *Cultivate Gratitude:* Regularly reflect on what you're thankful for to sustain a positive outlook.
- *Take Action Despite Fear:* Push through doubt with small, courageous steps to build momentum.

BADASS PRACTICE: LEARN THE LANGUAGE OF KINDNESS

Learn a new language. Or become more fluent in your less-dominant language if you are already multilingual. The more people you can communicate with, the more you'll make yourself available for work opportunities. Learning other languages will also open you up to new people and cultures. A friend of mine recently took a volunteer vacation, where she taught English to orphaned children in Gaza, Ukraine, Liberia, and other violence-torn countries. She said she enjoyed every minute and wants to do this every year, as she loved working with the kids. As she told me this story, her smile was at least a mile wide!

AFFIRMATION STATION

I have a strong center.

Whatever comes my way,
I can handle and handle well.

My inner strength is my guide
through and to a happy life.

The Mindful Badass

Embracing a positive badass mindset empowers individuals to tackle challenges with confidence and resilience. This mindset fuels motivation, encouraging bold decision-making and creative problem-solving. With a positive outlook, setbacks become stepping stones, and self-doubt fades, replaced by a belief in one's limitless potential. It also inspires others, creating a ripple effect of optimism and grit. By cultivating this dynamic approach, anyone can unlock their inner strength and achieve extraordinary results in any endeavor.

- A positive badass mindset builds resilience, helping you bounce back from failures.
- It drives bold action, pushing you to take risks and seize opportunities.
- It enhances creativity, enabling you to come up with innovative solutions to complex problems.
- It fosters self-confidence, empowering you to trust your instincts and abilities.
- Positivity attracts like-minded individuals, building a supportive network of driven people.
- It fuels persistence, ensuring that you stay committed to long-term goals despite challenges.
- A badass mindset inspires others, amplifying your impact in personal and professional circles.

“There are so many great things in life; why dwell on negativity?”

—Zendaya, actress and singer

Don’t Be Judgmental; Be Kind Just Because You Can

It’s easy to judge others for their actions and take for granted those we love or meet in chance encounters. We sometimes get so caught up in our busy-ness that we forget that others are busy too, they have rough days just like us, and they benefit from our kindness just as we do theirs. Go out of your way to smile at strangers, say "Good morning" and "Thank you," pay a compliment, and listen attentively to someone who needs your ear. Do it because you can, because it feels great, and because it makes someone else feel good. Don’t worry about a thank-you in return; let a thank-you be a beautiful perk rather than an expectation.

Badass Practice: Look at Everything in a New Way

Simply reframe your perception: Each of us has had dreams that, for one reason or another, we do not achieve. And we may have made choices that were not the best. Yet, rather than allowing regret to overtake us, we must celebrate all the other goals we've accomplished and the positive choices we've made. Human nature so often leads us to perceive the one negative in a sea of positives. But we can retrain ourselves to learn the lessons embedded in our mistakes, allowing ourselves to feel pride in the beauty we are capable of. All it takes is a little shift. You'll see.

Here are some ways to get to it:

- Start a new project or revive an old idea.
- Spend time outside to boost creativity and mental clarity.
- Try freewriting or brainstorming to generate fresh ideas.
- Take on activities that encourage exploration and curiosity.
- Use the natural momentum of the season to set creative goals.
- Try something you've always wanted to do.
- Establish a morning routine that nurtures your mind, body, and spirit.

- Manage and minimize the things in your day that feel limiting or rigid.
- Plant something. Try an herb—I love growing basil—or a bright flowering plant.

"It's really that my expectations of what I'm capable of are holding me back from accepting who I am."

—Jessamyn Stanley, American yoga teacher, body positivity advocate, and writer

AFFIRMATION STATION

I am uniquely made.

I am full of positivity.

I see myself as beautiful.

Swap Out Comparison for Contentment

Your true power is in how you view yourself! So remind yourself every day that you are beautiful and that you can do all the hard things set in front of you. Yes, those women on your Instagram feed are beautiful, but hey, guess what? So are you! Whether you believe it or not, somebody is looking at you and feeling covetous of something about you or something you have in your life.

Jealous thinking clouds your consciousness with unnecessary negativity and lowers your self-esteem, not to mention your vibe. Change this perspective, remove yourself from that negative space, and view yourself the way that everyone else does: as a gorgeous being with endless possibilities ahead of her.

Let's kick these comparisons aside and replace them with gratitude and grace.

Ditch Comparison and Competitiveness for True Badassery

You're out there shining, but let's talk about something that can dim your glow: comparison and competitiveness. These sneaky habits are the opposite of badass—they pull you away from your unique power and into a cycle of self-doubt and stress. Instead of celebrating your own magic, they trick you into measuring yourself against others, as if there's only so much awesome to go around. Spoiler alert: There's plenty, and you've got your own special slice of it!

When you catch yourself eyeing someone else's success, looks, or life with a twinge of envy or a need to one-up them, pause. That urge to compare or compete clouds your confidence and steals your joy. It's like trying to run your race while staring at someone else's track—you'll trip every time. Being a badass means owning your journey, cheering for others, and knowing that their wins don't dim your shine. You're not here to outdo anyone; you're here to be your best self.

So how do you break free? Start with gratitude. Take a moment each day to celebrate *you*—your strengths, your quirks, your progress. Write down three things you love about yourself or your life. Maybe it's your killer laugh, your knack for making others feel seen, or the way you tackled a tough day with grace. This shifts your focus from what you think you lack to the abundance you already have.

Next, reframe how you see others. Instead of competitors, view them as inspiration. That woman crushing it at work? Let her motivate you to chase your own goals. Someone's style or confidence catching your eye? Use it as a spark to try something new. When you lift others up, you lift yourself up too—it's a vibe that radiates badass energy.

Finally, embrace collaboration over competition. Connect with women who inspire you, share ideas, and encourage each other. There's something incredibly powerful about a community of women rooting for one another. That's where true badassery lives—in showing up authentically, celebrating your unique gifts, and creating space for everyone to shine.

So let's kick comparison and competitiveness to the curb. You're not here to be better than anyone else—you're here to be the best version of *you*. With gratitude, grace, and a whole lot of heart, you're unstoppable. Keep shining, badass!

How to Own Your Awesomeness (and Celebrate Others Too!)

You're a one-of-a-kind masterpiece, and owning your awesomeness is the ultimate badass move. It's about embracing your unique spark while cheering on the brilliance of others. Here are six tips to help you shine bright and lift everyone up, all in true badass gratitude style!

Start with Self-Love: Kick off each day by celebrating *you*. Look in the mirror and name one thing you love about yourself—your courage, your smile, your unstoppable spirit. Write it down or say it out loud. This simple act roots you in confidence and sets a positive tone. When you're filled with self-love, you radiate a vibe that inspires others to embrace their own greatness too.

Own Your Strengths: You've got gifts that make you uniquely awesome. Maybe you're a problem-solver, a listener, or a creative spark. Take time to identify your strengths and lean into them! Try something new that showcases your talents, like leading a project or sharing your art. Owning your strengths doesn't just boost your confidence—it shows others they can step into their power too.

Ditch the Perfection Trap: Being a badass isn't about being perfect—it's about being real. Embrace your quirks and so-called flaws; they make you *you*. Let go of the need to have it all together, and laugh off the small stuff. When you show up authentically, you permit others to do the same, creating a ripple effect of genuine, awesome vibes.

Celebrate Others' Wins: A true badass lifts others up. When a friend nails a goal or shines bright, cheer her on! Send a heartfelt text, leave a kind comment, or just say, "You're killing it!" Celebrating others doesn't dim your light—it amplifies it. This generous spirit builds a community where everyone's awesomeness thrives, and that's the kind of energy that changes the world.

Set Boundaries with Grace: Owning your awesomeness means protecting your energy. Say no to things that drain you, and yes to what lights you up. Set boundaries kindly but firmly, like, "I'd love to help, but I need to prioritize this right now." This empowers you to shine fully and encourages others to respect their own needs, creating a cycle of mutual support.

Spread Gratitude Daily: Gratitude is your secret weapon for owning your awesomeness. Each day, jot down or share one thing you're thankful for about yourself and someone else. Maybe it's your resilience and a friend's kindness. This habit keeps you grounded in your worth and fosters connection. When you spread gratitude, you create a space where everyone feels seen, valued, and ready to shine.

Tap into Your Own Creativity

The urge to create is one of humanity's strongest driving forces. Some people hear it as a calling; others sense it as a need. For me, it is a restless desire to explore, a questing curiosity that knows no bounds.

Whether it means putting pen to paper, paintbrush to canvas, or fingers to keyboard, each creative act taps into the same basic instinct: the innate need to express, invent, and discover oneself. For many, being blocked or prevented from creating causes them to wither away or to die a little bit each day.

To create is to live!
And we must do it every day.

Be Ripsniptious!

Simply put, "ripsniptious" (rip-*snip*-shuss) can be used to express something or describe someone wonderful and highly spirited. Today, you will be ripsniptious and notice all of the other ripsniptious things around you. Let this be your word of the day, and let it embody and introduce others to the word "ripsniptious"! It's fun to say, isn't it? It's even better to be it. It is also a wonderful compliment, and I think you are pretty darn ripsnippant for reading this book!

AFFIRMATION STATION

I choose gratitude—even when it's hard.

I am not my negative thoughts;
I am the awareness that transforms them.

One moment of thanks
can rewrite a whole day.

I find the light even when shadows
try to settle in.

CHAPTER 5

Breaking Habits That Break You Down

"Self-love and self-respect are not linear. Forgive yourself in those moments of doubt."

—Imani Barbarin, American writer, public speaker, and disability rights activist

We all find ourselves with some habits that don't serve our lives. Breaking these habits is an important step on your path to gratitude. You're ready to live with more joy and purpose, and that starts with breaking habits that dim your shine—complaining, comparing, seeing the glass half empty, and feeling ungrateful because nothing's ever enough. These autopilot behaviors sneak into our lives, draining energy and clouding gratitude. But here's the good news: With awareness and intention, you can rewrite these patterns and step into a life of badass gratitude. Let's dive into why these habits hold you back and how to break free, with an upbeat, kindly vibe to light your way.

Complaining is a habit that feels like venting but builds a negativity trap. It's easy to grumble about traffic, a tough day, or a rude coworker, but each gripe trains your brain to spot flaws. A 2024 study reported on by TalentSmartEQ found that chronic complaining increases cortisol, fueling stress and dampening joy. Gratitude flips the script. Instead of "This day's awful," try "I'm thankful for my cozy coffee." It's not ignoring reality—it's choosing to focus on what uplifts you. Start small: Notice one complaint, pause, and then replace it with a thankful thought. Over time, this rewires your mind for positivity, making joy your default.

Feeling competitive with others—envying their wins or measuring your worth against theirs—steals your peace. Social media amplifies this, flashing highlight reels that scream, "You're not enough!" But comparison is a thief. It blinds you to your unique gifts and fosters resentment. Gratitude is the antidote. When envy creeps in, thank the universe for *its* success and *your* journey. Celebrate others' wins—send a "Congrats!" text—and reflect on your own blessings. This shifts your heart from scarcity to abundance, where everyone's light can shine.

The "half-empty" attitude—always seeing what's missing—keeps you stuck. Maybe you got a raise but fixate on how it's not enough, or you're healthy but dwell on a minor ache. This mindset breeds dissatisfaction, making happiness a moving target. Gratitude reframes the lens. Instead of "I wish I had more," try "I'm grateful for what I have."

Each night, write down three things that went well. This trains your brain to spot abundance, turning your half-full glass into an overflowing one.

Ungratefulness, where nothing feels like enough, is the root of these habits. It's chasing "more" without savoring "now." You might have a loving family but crave a bigger house, or a solid job but yearn for a fancier title. This chase blocks joy. Gratitude grounds you in the present. Thank your body for carrying you, your friends for laughing with you, and your challenges for teaching you. By appreciating what's here, you find contentment that no external win can match.

Breaking these habits starts with awareness. Autopilot thrives in the shadows—mindless scrolling, snapping at a loved one, or sighing over "bad luck." Pause and notice: "I'm complaining again." This mindfulness is your superpower. From there, choose intention. Replace a gripe with thanks, envy with celebration, and lack with appreciation. It's not instant, but each choice is a step toward purpose. Surround yourself with positive inputs—uplifting books, kind people, gratitude-focused podcasts—to reinforce your new mindset. And be gentle with yourself. Slipups happen; what matters is starting again.

Why does this matter? These habits break you down, sapping energy for your dreams. Complaining breeds stress, comparison fuels self-doubt, half-empty thinking dulls hope, and ungratefulness blinds you to life's gifts. But breaking them builds you up. You become resilient, connected, and joyful. You're not just surviving—you're thriving, living with purpose, and radiating gratitude that inspires others. By ditching these habits, you free your heart to chase what truly matters.

Sweet friend, you're not stuck. Each moment is a chance to choose gratitude over grumbling, celebration over comparison, and abundance over lack. Start today by noticing one habit, shifting it with a thankful thought, and watching your world brighten. You're crafting a life of joy, one intentional step at a time. You've got this, and I'm cheering you on!

Tips to Break Habits That Break You Down

- **PAUSE AND NAME THE HABIT:** Catch yourself complaining, comparing, or feeling ungrateful. Say, "I'm on autopilot." Awareness is the first step. Pause, breathe, and choose a new response to break the cycle.

- **REPLACE COMPLAINTS WITH THANKS:** When you want to gripe, swap it for gratitude. Instead of "This line's so slow," say "I'm thankful for this moment to breathe." Gratitude journaling cuts stress by 15 percent, per research. Try it daily to make positivity your go-to.

- **CELEBRATE OTHERS' WINS:** Feeling competitive? Send a heartfelt "Great job!" to someone succeeding. Thank the universe for its light and yours. Studies show that gratitude for others reduces envy by 20 percent. This shifts your heart from rivalry to connection, boosting joy.

- **REFRAME THE HALF-EMPTY GLASS:** Notice a "not enough" thought? Flip it: "I'm grateful for what I have." Write three things daily that spark joy—a meal, a smile, a sunset. Optimism rises 15 percent with this habit, per 2023 research, filling your glass with hope.

- **SAVOR THE PRESENT MOMENT:** Ungratefulness chases "more." Ground yourself now—thank your body, your breath, your surroundings. A 2024 study found that present-focused gratitude boosts contentment by 25 percent. Take five minutes daily to notice what's good, anchoring you in what's enough.

- **CURATE POSITIVE INPUTS:** Surround yourself with uplifting books, podcasts, or friends who spark gratitude. Limit negative media or toxic inputs. A 2023 study showed that positive environments increase motivation by 20 percent. Feed your mind joy to crowd out old habits.

- **PRACTICE MICRO-GRATITUDE:** Thank someone for small things—a coworker's help, a stranger's smile. These tiny acts build a gratitude habit. Research shows that small kindnesses boost happiness by 10 percent. Say "I appreciate you" daily to rewire your brain for connection.

- **REFLECT ON GROWTH:** When you slip into old habits, ask, "What did I learn?" Write one takeaway. Reflective thinking builds resilience, per 2024 studies. See setbacks as growth, not failure, and thank yourself for trying. This keeps you moving forward.

- **SET A GRATITUDE TRIGGER:** Link gratitude to a daily habit, like thanking life for something each time you brush your teeth. Cues strengthen habits, per research. This makes gratitude automatic, reducing space for complaining or comparison over time.

- **BE KIND TO YOURSELF:** Breaking habits takes time. If you grumble or compare, don't judge—just start again. Self-compassion boosts motivation by 15 percent, per 2023 studies. Thank yourself for your effort: "I'm grateful I'm growing." This gentle approach fuels lasting change and joy.

Let's Make It a Complaint-Free World

Go one day without complaining. Even better, go for a week. If this is hard for you to accomplish, it's time to make some changes in your life. Think positively, live in the present, and appreciate where you are and who you are. Today is a gift, so accept and embrace it. Will Bowen wrote a fantastic book on this very topic that I turn to when I need a reminder, as we all do now and again. My copy came with a bracelet, a simple way to monitor how often you complain that helps you track your progress toward becoming "complaint-free." Put on the bracelet, and every time you complain, switch it to the other wrist. The goal is to go twenty-one consecutive days without switching the bracelet. It is harder than you might think, and I was a bit shocked at what a complainer I turned out to be. It was a really good exercise for me—I highly recommend it. I benefited enormously, and I suspect those around me did too!

> "Like sunflowers, no matter where they are planted turn towards the sun, I too began turning in the direction that nourished me."
>
> *—Lalah Delia, American spiritual writer, certified spiritual practitioner, wellness educator, and founder*

Share the Good: Toot Your Horn!

Many women are way too self-effacing. Badass women are not. Instructions: Complete these statements when you are feeling neutral or good about yourself. Then, next time you notice you're feeling bad, take out your worksheet and read your answers, and notice how your mood changes.

1. I like myself when:
2. I'm an expert at:

3. I feel good about:
4. My friends would tell you I have a great:
5. My favorite place is:
6. I'm loved by:
7. People say I am a good:
8. I've been told I have pretty:

Extol Others as You Would Extol Yourself

Compliment someone today and mean it. A genuine compliment can boost someone's confidence, and that is a great feeling. If you like your coworker's blouse or new haircut (or both), tell her. Open and honest communication works wonders for developing relationships and makes everybody's day a little bit nicer. You can change the trajectory of someone's day/week/month by simply asking them, "Do you know how great you are?"

Catch People Doing Something Right (and Make Sure They Know It)

During difficult transitions, our natural tendency is often to resist change and grow rigid. In this state, we seem to only be able to focus on the negatives. We think about the despair that follows the death of a loved one but not the wonderful moments spent together celebrating their life. We think of the heartbreak of a relationship ending but not the exhilaration and freedom of being unattached. We might even scold our loved ones, our friends, or our coworkers for something minor while we wallow in similar negativity. But it is in these moments that gratitude can be used to alter this way of thinking.

Finding positives and accentuating them is the easiest way to turn those proverbial frowns upside down and gray skies back to blue. Try catching someone doing something right for a change, not something wrong. Giving praise for a job well done will lift up all parties involved.

> "Speak your mind, even if your voice shakes."
>
> *—Maggie Kuhn, American activist known for founding the Gray Panthers movement*

Start a "To Don't" List

Whatever no longer serves you or becomes what I call a "time vampire," add it to the list—and just stop doing it. I want to remind you that you are a badass, and you are completely awesome.

BADASS PRACTICE:
LISTENING IS AN ACT OF LOVE AND RESPECT

We don't always have to donate time and energy to other parts of the world. Sometimes help is needed much closer to home. Is a parent, sibling, spouse, friend, or coworker having a difficult time? Help lift their spirits by letting them experience that loving feeling. Invite them to coffee or dinner, surprise them with a simple gift, or take them somewhere they like. Lean forward and listen closely. Just listen.

"Follow what feels good in the moment, every moment, and it will lead you through a most excellent life."

—Jen Sincero, bestselling American author, motivational speaker, and success coach

You Can Do All Things (but Maybe You Don't Have To)

Dear You: First off, good job on getting through the year and tracking your life. I sincerely hope you found some of the ideas herein to be helpful and provided some tips and tools for sailing through your tasks and rocking the good self-care you so richly deserve. My hope is also that, in the process of tracking your habits, noting your successes, reflecting on your days, and how you use your time, you also start to figure out what you no longer need to do. Try editing your life. Less is more.

Try to figure out the tasks, busy work, and moments you could be using for something more important that adds meaning to your life.

We all do it, and I catch myself all the time doing something that is not going to move any needles, make a difference in my life or anyone else's, and is just not worth the time. Time is the single most valuable resource in your life, so it's incumbent upon all of us to use our precious time well. Give yourself permission to do less so you can do the things that will make you happy, bring you peace of mind, help you achieve your career and personal goals, and inspire you to embrace and celebrate your true self. And my parting idea is to make a different kind of list—one that I think will be liberating and invigorating.

AFFIRMATION STATION

I am no longer available for what drains me.

I release autopilot living and reclaim the steering wheel.

Every conscious choice I make is a rebellion against what no longer serves me.

I am building habits that honor the life I deserve.

CHAPTER 6

Five Minutes a Day Can Change Your Life

"Each day comes bearing its gifts. Untie the ribbon."

—Ann Ruth Schabacker, United States Air Force officer and lieutenant colonel

Are you tired of walking around with a heavy heart? Do you need more inspiration? Studies show—and experts counsel—that gratitude is a key component of our happiness. People who are grateful about events and experiences from the past, who celebrate the triumphs instead of focusing on the losses or disappointments, tend to be more satisfied in the present. Gratitude guru Rhonda Byrne writes, "With all that I have read and all that I have experienced in my own life using *The Secret*, the power of gratitude stands above everything else. If you do only one thing with the knowledge of this book, use gratitude until it becomes your way of life."

Jeffrey Zaslow, a columnist for *The Wall Street Journal*, wrote that there may be a positive by-product of the troubled economic times that followed the stock market crashes in recent years: a decrease in the urge to complain. "People who still have jobs are finding reasons to be appreciative. It feels unseemly to complain about not getting a raise when your neighbor is unemployed," he wrote. "Homeowners are unhappy that home values have fallen, but it's a relief to avoid foreclosure."

Gratitude not only lifts our spirits; it also floats our boats and moves us to do all kinds of things inspired by joy. Gratitude can help us transform our fears into courage, our anger into forgiveness, our isolation into belonging, and another's pain into healing. Saying "Thank you" every day will create feelings of love, compassion, and hope.

But the fact is, the art of living—for that is what we speak about when we speak of gratitude—isn't something that comes naturally to most people. Most of us need to work intentionally to increase the intensity, duration, and frequency of positive, grateful feelings—

a daunting challenge, indeed. To master the art of being a gratitude practitioner, take time for gratitude every day; that works for me, and it will work for you. You'll be glad and oh-so-thankful you did.

The Bigger the Badass, the More You Need Self-Care!

You can do all things if you have a plan!

You must start with tending to yourself because if you are worn down, depleted, or frazzled, you can't thrive, let alone enjoy your life. We women, especially, often fall into the habit of what I call "putting yourself at the back of your own bus." You put your partner and your kids first, your job first, your friends first. Maybe your pets even come ahead of your partner, but regardless of the order, you take care of everyone else's needs first; and once you're done with all that, you don't have the energy to do much for yourself.

Please don't wear yourself out and put your own needs on the back burner because, if you are completely depleted, you can't be at your peak in any area of life.

If you are at your BEST, you will make your loved ones (even the dog) happier because they see you smiling, flowing, and looking good. A happy you is better for everyone! You will live better and have more fun when you're rocking self-care.

Smart Self-Care for Badass Women

A thoughtful approach to your self-care is a game changer when you are striving to live boldly and authentically. Self-care ignites inner strength, enabling you to face challenges with unshakable confidence and optimism. This mindset transforms fear into fuel, turning dreams into reality through relentless determination and creative problem-solving. It cultivates resilience, allowing setbacks to become lessons rather than roadblocks. By embracing positivity and grit, you inspire those around you, fostering a community of empowerment and growth. With this dynamic approach, people not only achieve personal success but also redefine what's possible, living life on their own terms with passion and purpose. Good self-care for badass women is about nurturing mind, body, and spirit to sustain their fierce energy and resilience.

1. **Mental Wellness:** Practice mindfulness or meditation to manage stress. Journaling helps you process your emotions and set goals. Engage in hobbies or creative outlets for joy and balance.
2. **Physical Health:** Prioritize regular exercise (e.g., strength training, yoga, or kickboxing) to boost energy and confidence. Eat nutrient-rich foods and

stay hydrated. Aim for seven to eight hours of quality sleep to recharge.

3. **Emotional Strength:** Set boundaries to protect your energy. Surround yourself with supportive, uplifting people. Therapy or coaching can provide tools for emotional resilience.
4. **Personal Growth:** Invest in learning—read books, take courses, or attend workshops to fuel ambition. Celebrate wins, big or small, to reinforce confidence.
5. **Rest and Play:** Schedule downtime to avoid burnout. Treat yourself to fun experiences, like travel, spa days, or dancing, to spark joy.

Say no without guilt to energy-draining commitments.

"Extraordinary things are always hiding in places people never think to look."

—Jodi Picoult, bestselling American author

BADASS PRACTICE: MAKE TIME FOR GRATITUDE EVERY DAY

When you begin a daily practice of recognizing the positive events that occur and the pleasant encounters you have with others, you will start being more thankful. Perhaps it's someone who holds the door for you at the supermarket, the nice conversation you have with a stranger while at the coffee shop, or a hug with someone you love. These are the small moments, often the ones we forget. Savor their beauty and what they tell you about humankind—that we do live among many good people.

Weeding Therapy

I joke to my friends that, if I didn't go out and weed the garden every day, I might be on a gurney or in a rubber room. When things go wrong by midmorning, there's only one thing to do: Head for the garden. Maybe the beans need weeding. Great—something to work out my resentments on. I kneel and start; the lamb's-quarters and pigweed come out easily, so I rip them out angrily, in big handfuls. That feels good. After a few minutes, I am enjoying the comforting feel of the soft, warm earth.

I notice that the tiny beans are coming along just as they should, in elegant clusters hanging straight down.

As the weed heap grows and the row of handsome, weed-free plants extends behind me, I realize I'm not frowning anymore; actually, I'm smiling.

Is gardening therapeutic? You bet it is.

Be Good in Your Own Neighborhood

Pick up and recycle or compost loose garbage as you walk. Sidewalks are meant for safe walking, not weaving through someone else's abandoned bottles and crumpled take-out bags. Take pride in the area you live in, and help contribute to keeping it clean and safe. One person helping can inspire many others to do the same. I vowed to do this fifteen years ago while living in the Lower Haight in San Francisco. By the end of each week, I usually had a big bag to take to the HANC Recycling Center. I've gotten some puzzled glances and even laughter when dressed up for a meeting and walking down the street picking up garbage, empty bottles, and what-have-you. I will occasionally say, "This is my service to the earth. Recycling is my religion." And it is. I have the planet's back!

"Life is measured in love and positive contributions and moments of grace."

—Carly Fiorina, American CEO, businesswoman, and politician

Share Your Awesomeness with the World!

This is your life! Only *you* can truly control your choices. Choosing happiness is the best way to achieve being good to yourself as well as the world. Here are some suggestions for how you can guarantee simple joy in your life:

- Be the best you can be by your own standards.
- Surround yourself with people who inspire you and make you feel good.
- Focus on what you have, not what you lack.
- Remember that optimism trumps pessimism every time!
- Smile often and genuinely.
- Be honest with yourself and those in your world.
- Help others.
- Embrace your past, live in the present, and look forward to what is yet to come.

BADASS PRACTICE:
ADD A HALF HOUR TO YOUR DAY

This is one of the most brilliant and simple pieces of advice and one of my all-time best "life hacks." Wake up a half hour earlier each day and use those thirty minutes to reach out to people. It can be as easy as wishing a happy birthday to your Facebook contacts, making one meaningful phone call first thing in the morning, or writing a personal note to someone you have been meaning to get in contact with. I remember thinking I really didn't want to get up any earlier; my days were long enough. But this slight change has been absolutely transformative. It is a kind of self-care too, because it lifts my heart and spirit as few other things can. The extra half hour of every morning has been one of the most valuable investments I have ever made—so much so that I made it an hour. It completely changed my life for the better. Try it!

Make a list of what you'll do with that extra half hour tomorrow.

BADASS PRACTICE: GET GROUNDED, LITERALLY

I love that Earth is coming into vogue as more and more people realize the need to spend time with nature. You don't need to go to a mountaintop to get in touch with Mother Earth; try your own backyard, explore a nearby park, or visit a farm. Whichever you choose, make sure it is a dry, sunny, and warm day. Just take yourself and a blanket. Find a place that looks right and that you are drawn to, and set your blanket and any belongings down so that you're holding nothing. Remove your shoes and stand on the earth itself. Wiggle your toes to feel the soil underneath you. Feel free to spend as much time as you like in your earthing space. Commune with nature safely in the embrace of Mother Earth.

Grab your gratitude journal and write down when and where you plan to practice earthing.

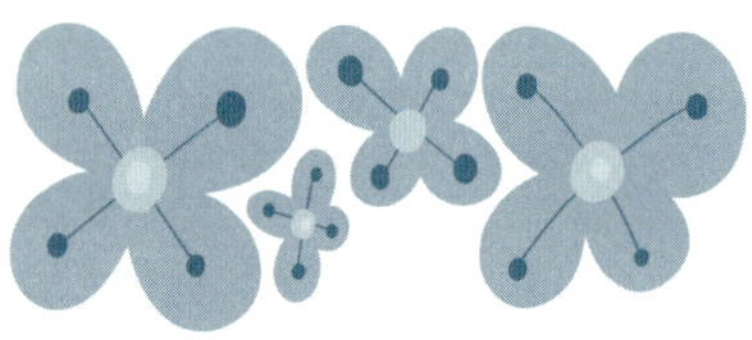

Self-Belief: Your Gratitude Superpower

Self-belief is a secret superpower that makes gratitude even more powerful—it's the spark that turns "I'm thankful" into "I've got this." When you believe in yourself, you start seeing every challenge as a chance to grow, and gratitude becomes your fuel to keep going. I learned this the hard way during a rough patch some years ago. I'd just moved to a new city with big dreams but zero connections. I felt like a tiny fish in a huge pond, and my self-doubt was loud. Then, one morning, I looked in the mirror and said, "I'm grateful for my courage to try." That simple act of believing in my own bravery shifted everything—I started networking, landed a gig, and built a life I love.

Self-belief lets you be grateful for you—your strength, your quirks, your journey. It's not about being perfect; it's about trusting that you're enough, even on the messy days. When you pair that with gratitude, you're unstoppable. You start thanking yourself for showing up, for learning, and for daring to dream. And that energy? It's contagious.

Emit Good Vibes

Take stock of your day-to-day life. Are you giving to others, or is there an imbalance? Do your work and your immediate family get 99 percent of what you offer the world? You can change that in one day. Donate more of your time or money to a charity. Supporting a cause will help keep you informed about social issues and can strengthen your sense of well-being while benefiting others in the process. What you give, even if it is simply positive thoughts, will come back to you tenfold.

BADASS PRACTICE: THE SELF-BELIEF MIRROR MOMENT

Stand in front of a mirror each morning over the course of a week. Look yourself in the eyes and say, "I'm grateful for my [fill in the blank]." Maybe it's your resilience, your sense of humor, or your kind heart. Then add, "I believe in myself to achieve [your goal or dream]." Write down how you feel afterward. On day seven, share this practice with a friend—encourage them to try it too. You'll both feel the glow of self-belief and gratitude lifting you up. You're a powerhouse, even when you don't feel like it. Believing in yourself is the ultimate thank-you to your own spirit. What will you thank yourself for today?

Teaching Gratitude

Teach your children well. Sit down with your child and ask him or her to create a mantra about thankfulness. Provide a simple starting point: "Thank you for . . ." Then ask your child to draw a picture to go with the concept and get started writing the first of MANY thank-you notes for years to come!

Be Thankful for Everyday Wins

Life isn't always full of big shiny victories, but it's the tiny wins that can light up your day. I learned this on a rainy Tuesday a few years back, when I was feeling totally blah. I'd spilled coffee on my favorite shirt, my inbox was a mess, and I was just over it. But then I noticed something: The barista at my local coffee spot had slipped an extra cookie in my bag with a smiley face drawn on the wrapper. That little act of kindness hit me hard. I sat down, munched on that cookie, and thought, "Thank you for this moment." It wasn't much, but it was enough to shift my whole day.

Badass Gratitude is about celebrating these everyday wins—the warm sun on your face, a text from a friend, or even just making it out of bed when you didn't want to. These moments are your quiet cheerleaders, reminding you that joy hides in the small stuff.

"Whatever you want to do, if you want to be great at it, you have to love it and be able to make sacrifices for it."

—Maya Angelou, American poet, singer, memoirist, and civil rights activist

BADASS PRACTICE:
THE DAILY WIN JAR

Grab a jar (or any container you love) and some scraps of paper. Each day, write down one tiny win you're grateful for—like "I laughed at a silly meme," or "I took a deep breath and felt okay." Drop it in the jar. At the end of the week, share your favorite win with a friend or family member. Let them add one of theirs too. You'll be amazed by how these little records of gratitude stack up and lift everyone's spirits.

What's your tiny win today?

AFFIRMATION STATION

I make time for gratitude.

I deserve five minutes of stillness every single day.

My day begins with intention and ends with peace.

I always find moments to ground, breathe, and give thanks.

CHAPTER 7

Staying Thankful in Difficult Times

"Pain is important: how we evade it, how we succumb to it, how we deal with it, how we transcend it."

—Audre Lorde, American writer, womanist, radical feminist, and philosopher

Grief and hard times can hit like a rogue wave—messy, overwhelming, and often uninvited. Yet, even in the thick of it, gratitude can be a lifeline: not some Pollyanna fluff but a gritty, badass tool to keep you grounded. It's not about slapping a smile on pain or pretending everything's fine; it's about finding slivers of light in the dark, sassy-sweet style. Here's how to approach grief and tough moments with gratitude that's real, raw, and resilient.

First, let yourself feel the suck. Grief isn't a Pinterest board of inspirational quotes—it's snotty cries, rage, and existential dread. Trying to "be grateful" without honoring the hurt is like putting lipstick on a pig. So scream, sob, or punch a pillow. Then, when you're ready, shift your lens just a smidge. Gratitude doesn't erase pain; it coexists with it. Start small: Maybe you're grateful for the friend who texted "I'm here" or the coffee that got you out of bed. These aren't grand gestures—they're tiny anchors in the storm.

Next, reframe the narrative without sugarcoating it. Hard times are brutal, but they often reveal what matters. Lost a job? It's okay to hate it, but maybe you're grateful for the nudge to chase a dream you shelved. Mourning a loved one? The ache is proof of love—gratitude can live in memories that still spark joy, like their terrible dance moves or late-night talks. This isn't toxic positivity; it's acknowledging the mess while spotting the lessons or love woven into it. Be sassy about it: Tell the universe, "Yeah, this hurts, but I'm still here, and I see the good stuff too."

Lean into rituals that ground you. Gratitude needs roots, especially when life feels like a dumpster fire. Write down three things each day that didn't totally suck—maybe a stranger's smile, a warm shower, or the fact you didn't cry during a work meeting. Or try a gratitude jar: Scribble moments of grace on scraps of paper, and toss them in. On brutal days, dump it out and read them. It's a sassy act of defiance against despair, reminding you that, even in chaos, there's something worth holding on to.

Connect with others because gratitude thrives in community. Share your pain with someone who gets it—grief shared is grief softened. Then, notice the people who show up: the coworker who covers your shift, the neighbor who drops off soup. Say thanks, even if it's just a nod or a quick text. Expressing gratitude builds bridges, and those bridges keep you from drowning. Plus, it's pretty sweet to realize you're not as alone as you feel.

Finally, give yourself grace. Some days, gratitude will feel like a stretch, and that's okay. You're not failing; you're human. Hard times don't come with a gratitude quota. If all you've got is "I'm grateful I survived today," that's enough. Be kind to your weary heart, and sassy toward the idea that you've got to be perfect.

Gratitude in grief isn't about fixing the pain—it's about finding a way to breathe through it. It's a middle finger to despair, a wink at hope, and a promise that, even in the hardest times, there's something worth seeing. Keep it real, keep it small, and let it carry you forward, one badass step at a time.

BADASS PRACTICE: FIND ONE THING TO HANG ON TO

When life feels like too much, stop for a moment. Find one thing—just one—you're grateful for right now. It could be "I'm grateful for this cup of tea," or "I'm grateful I'm still trying." Write it down on your phone or a scrap of paper. Then, share that gratitude with someone you trust—maybe a quick text or a call. Let them share one of theirs too. You'll feel a little lighter knowing that you're not alone in the storm.

Chaos can't dim your shine forever, sweet soul. Gratitude is your anchor, helping you find light even on the hardest days. What's your light today?

"Gratitude paints little smiley faces on everything it touches."

—Richelle E. Goodrich, American author, poet, and philosopher

Affirmations: Your Gratitude Booster

Affirmations are little love notes to your soul—they remind you of your worth and amplify your gratitude in the most beautiful way. When you pair affirmations with gratitude, you're not just saying "Thank you" for what's around you; you're also saying "Thank you" to yourself for showing up. I discovered this a few summers ago when I was feeling stuck. I'd been rejected from a job I really wanted, and my confidence was shaky. One morning, I wrote on a sticky note: "I'm grateful for my persistence, and I'm capable of amazing things." I stuck it on my laptop and repeated it daily. Slowly, I started noticing more to be thankful for—like my determination, my creativity, and the support of my friends. That affirmation didn't just lift my spirits; it helped me land an even better gig!

Affirmations work because they rewire your mindset. They take your gratitude practice from "I'm thankful for this moment" to "I'm thankful for *me* in this moment." They build a bridge between where you are and where you want to be, all while keeping you grounded in appreciation for the journey.

BADASS PRACTICE:
THE AFFIRMATION ANCHOR

Pick one gratitude-focused affirmation that feels right for you, like "I'm grateful for my strength, and I'm growing every day." Write it on a colorful sticky note and place it somewhere you'll see it—like your mirror or notebook. Say it out loud each morning for a week; then share it with a loved one. Ask them to create their own affirmation, and swap stories about how it feels. You'll both feel the warmth of gratitude and self-love growing stronger.

Affirmations are your daily reminder that you're a gift, and so is your journey. What affirmation will you choose to boost your gratitude today?

Staying Grateful in the Thick of It

Life can throw you some serious curveballs—job loss, heartbreak, or a bank account screaming for mercy. But here's the thing: Badass gratitude isn't just a warm fuzzy; it's a steel-toed boot that kicks despair in the teeth. When times get tough, staying thankful keeps you grounded, like a scrappy Appalachian girl who's just moved to California and realized a slice of pizza costs more than her pride. That was me, fresh out of grad school, landing in San Francisco with big dreams and a wallet that laughed at me.

Picture this: I'm living in a converted closet in a gloriously grungy Victorian on Haight Street. Rent's eating my paycheck, gas for the Bay Bridge commute is a luxury, and food? Let's just say I'm eyeing the pigeons like they're dinner. My mama raised me to never borrow a dime, so when my budget shrank to pennies, I bought a bag of apples and a sack of potatoes with my last coins. For two weeks, I lived on that and herbal tea, dreaming of the day I'd have my own place in the Lower Haight. It wasn't glamorous—my stomach growled louder than a Muni bus—but I was hell-bent on making it.

Those apples and potatoes weren't just food; they were my rebellion against giving up. Every bite was a middle finger to defeat. I'd sit in my closet-room, sipping tea, and think, "I'm still here, universe. Watch me." Gratitude wasn't about pretending I loved my spud diet; it was about being thankful for the fire in my gut that kept me going. I was grateful for the job that would eventually pay me, for the strangers who became friends, and for the stubborn streak Mama had drilled into me. Those slivers of light kept me from crumbling.

When I finally scraped together enough for first, last, and a security deposit on a larger place, I felt like Rocky Balboa dancing at the top of those Philly steps. No, I didn't fight Apollo Creed, but I'd fought my own fight—pinching pennies, eating the same damn meal, and believing I'd make it. That tiny apartment was my victory ring, a cozy nook to share with new pals and old loves. I was so darn proud, not just for surviving but for thriving in my own scrappy way.

Gratitude in hard times isn't about faking joy. It's about spotting the small wins: the friend who texts "You got this," the sunrise that doesn't care about your bank balance, or the fact that you're still standing. It's sassy because it says, "Life, you're tough, but I'm tougher." It's sweet because it softens the edges, reminding you of the good still hanging around. Those two weeks of apples and potatoes taught me that, even when life's a dumpster fire, there's always something to hold on to—a lesson, a laugh, or a spark of pride.

Now, I'm not saying it's easy. Some days, gratitude feels like lifting a boulder. But even then, you can be thankful for the strength to try. Whether it's a roof over your head, a memory that makes you smile, or just the fact that you didn't cry in public, those moments are your anchors. They're proof that you're badass enough to keep going, to dance at the top of your own steps, savoring the triumph of making it through. So when life gets heavy, dig deep, find your gratitude, and let it carry you to your next Rocky moment.

"I'm choosing happiness over suffering, I know I am. I'm making space for the unknown future to fill up my life with yet-to-come surprises."

—Elizabeth Gilbert,
American journalist and author

Gratitude Adjustments

TIP 1: FEEL THE PAIN, THEN FIND THE SPARK: Hard times hurt like hell—job loss, grief, and an empty fridge don't play nice. Don't fake a smile; let yourself cry, curse, or eat ice cream for dinner. But once you've aired out the hurt, look for a spark of good. When I was broke in San Francisco, living on apples and potatoes, I was as mad as a wet cat. Yet I was thankful for my job, even if payday felt like it was a million years away. That spark kept me going. Start small: Maybe it's the friend who listens to your rants or the fact that you got out of bed. Write down one thing each day that doesn't suck. It's not about ignoring the pain; it's about proving there's still light. My closet-room on Haight Street was cramped, but it was mine, and that fueled my gratitude. Be sassy—tell life, "You hit hard, but I see the good stuff." Be sweet—let those sparks remind you that you're not alone. Over time, those tiny notes build a ladder out of the dark, showing you that you're tougher than the toughest storms.

TIP 2: REFRAME THE STRUGGLE AS A STORY: Every hard time is a chapter, not the whole book. When I was pinching pennies for a bag of spuds, I felt like a failure. But looking back, it's a story of grit—I'm the dark horse who made it to her own apartment. Reframing doesn't mean sugarcoating; it's seeing the lesson or strength in the mess. Lost a loved one? The pain's real, but gratitude lives in memories of their laugh. Jobless? It sucks, but maybe it's a push toward a dream. Jot down what the struggle's teaching you: patience, courage, or how to make a mean potato soup. My two weeks of apples taught me I could outlast anything. Be sassy—call your struggle a plot twist, not a tragedy. Be sweet—cherish the growth it brings. Your story's still being written, and gratitude helps you pen a comeback worth celebrating.

TIP 3: BUILD A GRATITUDE RITUAL: Gratitude needs a home, especially when life's a mess. Create a ritual to make it stick. When I was broke, I'd sip tea and list three things I was thankful for: a warm bed, a kind coworker, or just surviving the day. Try a gratitude bowl—scribble good moments on paper and toss them in. On bad days, read them and remember the wins. My giving bowl would've had notes like "paid rent!" or "found a cheap diner!" It's a sassy way to say, "I'm still kicking." Or set a phone reminder to pause and think of one good thing. Be sweet—let these rituals ground you. They don't fix everything, but they're a daily reminder that, even in chaos, there's something worth holding on to. My potato days proved that rituals turn sparks into flames, keeping you warm through the coldest times.

TIP 4: LEAN ON YOUR PEOPLE: No one gets through hard times alone. When I was scraping by in San Francisco, friends who shared their leftovers or invited me for coffee were my lifelines. Reach out—share your struggle with someone who gets it. Then, notice who shows up: the pal who calls, the neighbor with cookies. Say thanks, even if it's a quick "You're a gem." Gratitude for others builds bridges, and those bridges keep you out of deep water. I was thankful for the coworker who slipped me a granola bar when I looked hangry. Be sassy—call your crew your VIPs. Be sweet—let their kindness soften the hurt. Connection fuels resilience, and gratitude for your people is like a warm hug in a cold world. My *Rocky* moment came because others cheered me on, proving we're stronger together.

TIP 5: CELEBRATE THE SMALL WINS: Hard times make every step feel like climbing Mt. Everest. Celebrate the tiny victories—they're your fuel. When I bought that bag of apples, it wasn't just food; it was me saying, "I'm not quitting." Paid a bill? High-five yourself. Got through a day without crying? That's a win. Keep a mental or written tally of these moments. My win was saving enough for my apartment, but even making it to payday was huge. Be sassy—strut like you just won an Oscar for Best Survivor. Be sweet—give yourself credit for showing up. These wins stack up, building momentum. My two weeks of spuds were a string of small victories that led to my own place. Gratitude for them is like cheering your inner underdog, pushing you toward bigger triumphs.

TIP 6: GIVE YOURSELF GRACE: Some days, gratitude feels impossible, and that's okay. You're not a robot; you're a human in a rough patch. When I was tired of potatoes, I didn't always feel thankful—sometimes I just felt pissed. Don't beat yourself up if you can't muster a "glass-half-full" vibe. Be grateful for the effort, for still being here. My grace was knowing I'd tried my best, even when I was cranky. Be sassy—tell the world, "I'm doing me, flaws and all." Be sweet—treat yourself like you'd treat a friend. Rest, binge a show, or eat that extra cookie. My *Rocky* moment wasn't perfect; it was real. Gratitude for your own resilience, even when it's messy, is the ultimate badass move, carrying you through to brighter days.

When You Find Yourself in a Lonely Place

Loneliness can feel like a heavy fog settling over your heart when life gets hard. I've been there—when I moved to San Francisco, a stranger in a new city, those moments felt like my world was unraveling, but here's the truth: You're not alone in feeling this way, and you have the power to shift the tide.

With a gentle dose of badass gratitude, you can turn loneliness into connection, helplessness into purpose, and isolation into a life filled with joy and new bonds. This isn't about ignoring the ache—it's about honoring it, then taking small, bold steps to weave gratitude and kindness into your days. Inspired by my work for the Random Acts of Kindness team, which sparked a global movement (and some bestselling books), here's how to embrace gratitude to rebuild your world, one heartfelt connection at a time. You've got this, and every step forward is a win.

Gratitude isn't a magic fix, but it's quiet strength that helps you see the light through the fog. It's about noticing the people, moments, and possibilities already in your orbit and using them to lift yourself up. When I was alone in San Francisco, gratitude for a neighbor's wave or a stranger's kind word became my lifeline. After my fiancé's death, writing down one thing each day that brought me comfort—like a friend's text or a warm cup of tea—

helped me find my footing. These aren't grand gestures; they're small acts of courage that remind you that the world is still full of goodness. By leaning into gratitude, you're not just surviving loneliness—you're opening doors to new friendships, purpose, and joy. Following are six ways to infuse your life with connection and gratitude, making every step feel like a gift to yourself and others.

"There is nothing stronger than a broken woman who has rebuilt herself."

—Hannah Gadsby, Australian comedian, writer, author, and actor

How You Can Connect and Cultivate New Relationships

REACH OUT WITH INTENTION: Think of someone you miss—an old friend, a family member, or even a colleague who always made you smile. Make a list of these people, adding names as they pop into your mind. Each day, pick one person and reach out—call, text, or invite them for a walk or coffee. I started doing this in San Francisco, calling friends I hadn't spoken to in years, and those conversations rekindled bonds that warmed my heart. Plan something simple to do together, like grabbing a pastry or strolling in a park. Gratitude for these connections grows when you nurture them, and each call is a step toward a fuller life.

VOLUNTEER FOR A CAUSE YOU CARE ABOUT: What matters to you? Whether it's animals, kids, or the environment, find a way to give back. Volunteering connects you with people who share your passions. When I joined a local political campaign, I met incredible folks and felt grateful for the chance to make a difference. Look for opportunities in your community—soup kitchens, animal shelters, or library programs. The gratitude you feel for contributing will spark new friendships and a sense of purpose, turning loneliness into belonging.

EMBRACE PLAYFUL MOMENTS: Play is a gratitude booster. Invite friends for a game night with classics, like Scrabble or Uno; or join a local group for activities, like hiking or water aerobics. I once threw a spontaneous block party in my neighborhood, and the laughter and shared stories filled me with gratitude for my community. Check out live music at a local spot, and dance like nobody's watching. These moments of joy remind you that life is still vibrant, opening your heart to new connections.

LEARN SOMETHING NEW: Sign up for a class you've always wanted to try—painting, cooking, or even community theater. I found free art classes at a local college and felt grateful for every brushstroke that brought me out of my shell. Join a community choir or a pottery workshop. Learning alongside others builds bonds and fuels gratitude for your own growth. Each new skill is a reminder of your resilience and a door to meeting kindred spirits.

JOIN OR START A BOOK CLUB: Book clubs are a gold mine for connection. Find one that matches your interests—mysteries, memoirs, or travel books—or start your own. I joined a book group through a women's organization and found some of my closest friends there. Discussing stories over coffee or wine creates shared gratitude for ideas and camaraderie. It's a simple way to feel connected and inspired, turning lonely evenings into lively conversations.

TAKE ONE STEP TODAY: Loneliness can make staying home feel easier, but one small action can shift everything. Write down one person you'd love to reconnect with or one activity you're curious about. Then do it—send that text, sign up for that class, or show up to a community event. After my fiancé's passing, I forced myself to call a friend for coffee, and that single step—reaching out, hearing from someone who loved me—sparked gratitude for the support I didn't realize was waiting. Each action is a seed of gratitude that grows into new connections and possibilities.

Why It Works: These tips weave gratitude and kindness into your life without feeling forced. They're about taking small, brave steps to reconnect with others and yourself, turning loneliness into a chance to build something beautiful. Each call, volunteer shift, or playful moment is a way to say, "I'm thankful for the people and possibilities still here." By embracing these acts, you're not just easing loneliness—you're creating a life rich with joy, purpose, and new possibilities. Start today, even with one tiny step, and watch gratitude transform your world.

Let Your Love Shine

RANDOM ACTS OF LOVING-KINDNESS: The following are some ideas for you to consider that celebrate love. Love isn't all about romance; it includes everyone who touches your heart: Relatives, coworkers, neighbors, good friends, your children, and even strangers. As they say, love makes the world go 'round.

"I JUST CALLED TO SAY I LOVE YOU": Call your parents (or whoever helped raise you), and thank them for everything they did for you!

HELP THE HELPERS: Servicemen and -women are doing just that: SERVICE. And they should be thanked for it. Many of these noble souls are very far away and receive little mail to their camps or barracks. Take a few moments to acknowledge their contributions, and offer a friendly hello from back home in the USA. You can learn all about Operation Gratitude at www.operationgratitude.com.

LOVE NOTES: Leave encouraging, inspiring, or funny notes/quotes in a library book or other random places (without littering or defiling public property). A simple note stapled to a bulletin board, taped to a column, or written in chalk on the sidewalk may influence others in wonderful ways—and bring happiness to others.

Ten Mood-Boosting Tools for Handling Worry, Anxiety, and Tough Times

1. **CRAFT PERSONAL AFFIRMATIONS:** Write affirmations that resonate with your heart, like "I am worthy of joy," or "I release what I can't control." Make them specific to your struggles. Repeat them daily, aloud or silently, to reframe negative thoughts and build confidence.

2. **PAIR AFFIRMATIONS WITH BREATHING:** When worry spikes, inhale deeply for four counts, hold, then exhale for six. As you breathe, say, "I am calm and capable." This combo soothes your nervous system, grounding you in the present and easing anxious thoughts.

3. **MOVE YOUR BODY, LIFT YOUR MOOD:** Exercise releases endorphins, which combat depression. Try a ten-minute walk or dance session while repeating, "I am strong." Even gentle movement shifts energy, helping affirmations sink in and reminding you of your body's resilience.

4. **JOURNAL YOUR WINS:** Each night, write down three things you did well, no matter how small, alongside an affirmation such as "I am growing." This counters self-criticism, boosts self-esteem, and helps you see progress, even on tough days filled with sadness.

5. **CREATE A SAFE SPACE:** Designate a cozy corner with blankets, candles, or music. Sit there to say affirmations such as "I am safe." This space will become a sanctuary, reducing worry and offering comfort when you're feeling down or overwhelmed.

6. **LIMIT SOCIAL MEDIA OVERLOAD:** Endless scrolling can fuel comparison and sadness. Set boundaries, like limiting your scroll time to thirty minutes daily, and affirm, "I am enough as I am." This protects your mental space, helping you focus on your own worth and peace.

7. **CONNECT WITH YOUR TRIBE:** Share your feelings with a trusted friend or support group. Say, "I am supported" before reaching out. Connection reduces isolation, making depression and worry feel less heavy and reminding you that you're not alone.

8. **PRACTICE SELF-COMPASSION BREAKS:** Pause during tough moments, place a hand on your heart, and say, "I am kind to myself." This softens self-judgment, eases depressive thoughts, and nurtures the love you deserve, especially when worry feels relentless.

9. **SET TINY, ACHIEVABLE GOALS:** Break tasks into small steps, like "Make my bed" or "Drink water." Affirm, "I am capable of progress." Completing these tasks builds momentum, countering inertia and giving you tangible proof of your strength.

10. **SEEK PROFESSIONAL SUPPORT:** Therapists or counselors can guide you through depression, anxiety, and worry. Affirm, "I am brave for seeking help." Professional tools, paired with affirmations, empower you to navigate challenges with clarity and resilience, reinforcing your inner badass.

AFFIRMATION STATION

I hold grief and gratitude in the same hands.

There is always something to be thankful for.

I am stronger than what I'm walking through.

Gratitude is my anchor.

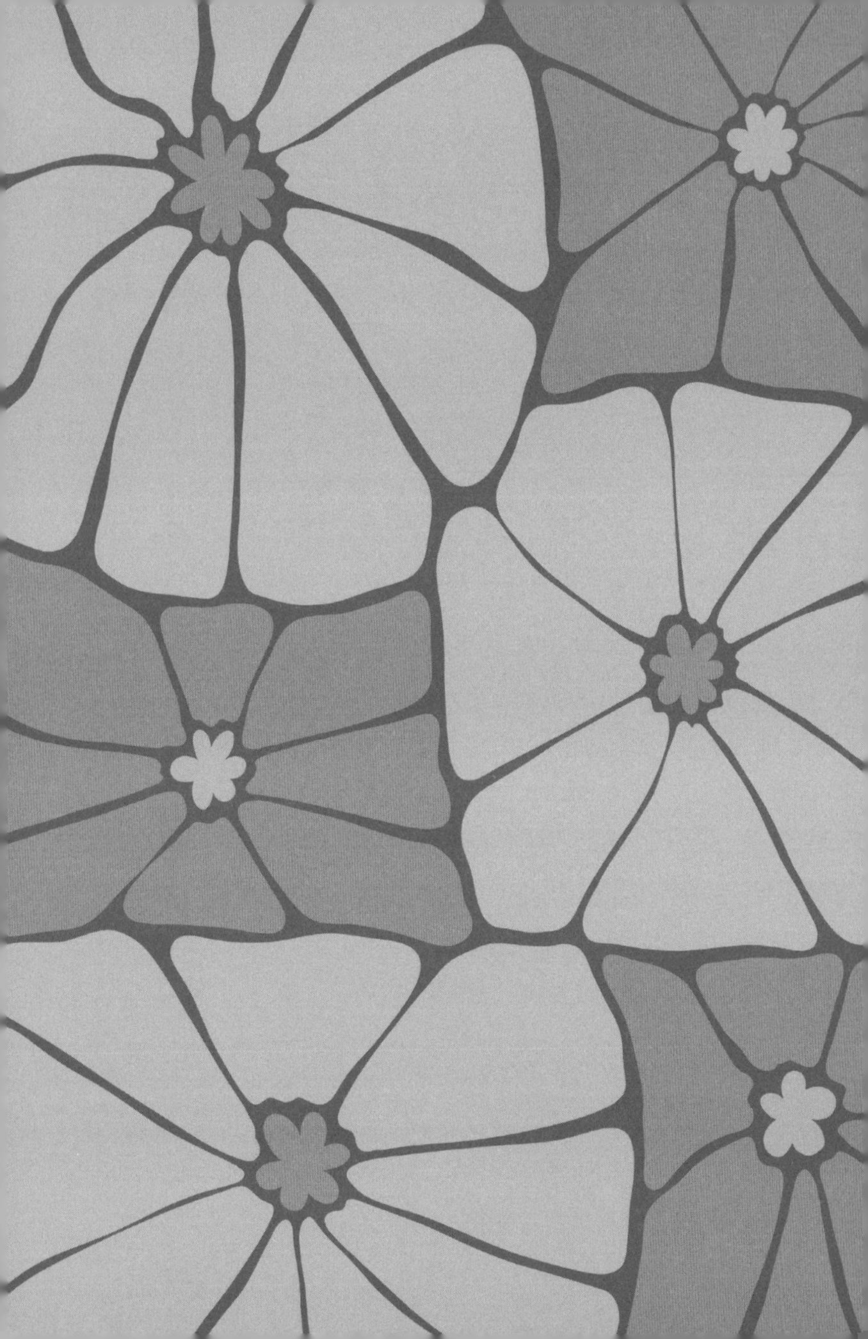

CHAPTER 8

Start Counting Your Blessings, Literally

"If you can't dream big, ridiculous dreams, what's the point in dreaming at all?"

—Ronda Rousey, American professional wrestler, actress, judoka, and mixed martial artist

Gratitude isn't just a warm, fuzzy feeling; it's a superpower, a vibrant force that rewires your heart and mind for a life brimming with joy, grace, and success. It's the art of counting your blessings, not just when life feels like a sunlit meadow but even when it's a stormy slog. Embracing gratitude transforms the mundane into the miraculous, turning everyday moments into opportunities for growth and happiness. It's practical, poetic, and profoundly badass. Here's why cultivating a gratitude practice is the cornerstone of a fulfilling life and how you can make it your own. Counting your blessings has a magical effect; it generates more blessings!

At its core, gratitude is about noticing the good—however small—and letting it anchor you. It's pausing to thank the barista who made your coffee just right or appreciating the crisp morning air on your walk to work. These micro-moments of acknowledgment build a mindset that sees abundance where others see lack. When I first moved to California, I was steeped in a scarcity mindset, fretting over every bill. But, inspired by Louise Hay's wisdom and catalyzed by my friend Duncan, I began a simple ritual: thanking the utility company as I paid my bills. "Thank you for the light in my home," I'd say, sealing the envelope with a smile. It wasn't just about paying on time (though that helped my credit score); it was about shifting my perspective from dread to appreciation. That shift felt like alchemy, turning financial stress into a celebration of provision.

Gratitude works because it rewires your brain. Neuroscience backs this up: Studies show that practicing gratitude increases dopamine and serotonin, the feel-good chemicals that boost mood and resilience. It's like a mental gym session—each thank-you strengthens your positivity muscle, making it easier to find joy even on tough days. And the best part? It's free, takes seconds, and compounds like interest in a happiness bank.

Why Gratitude Leads to a Happy Life

A life rooted in gratitude is a life full of grace and possibility. When you count your blessings, you're not ignoring life's challenges; you're choosing to see the light among them. This doesn't mean slapping a smile on pain—it means acknowledging what's good when things are tough. Maybe your car broke down, but you're grateful for the friend who gave you a ride. Maybe work is stressful, but you're thankful for the paycheck that keeps you afloat. This balance fosters resilience, the kind that carries you through storms with poise.

Gratitude also magnetizes success. When you approach life with an attitude of abundance, opportunities seem to multiply. People are drawn to your positivity; doors open because you're open to them. When I met Louise Hay at a trade show, my heart pounding as I thanked her for her teachings, her warmth and generosity—gifting me signed books—amplified my gratitude, creating a ripple effect of joy and connection. That moment wasn't just luck; it was the universe reflecting the energy I'd been cultivating. Gratitude sets off a chain reaction: The more you give, the more you receive.

Practical Steps to Live with Badass Gratitude

Building a gratitude practice doesn't require a guru or a retreat—just intention and a few minutes a day. Here are practical, poetic ways to make counting your blessings a habit:

- *Morning Gratitude Kickstart:* Start your day by listing three things you're thankful for. Maybe it's the sunrise, your cozy bed, or the fact that you woke up. Write them down or say them aloud to set a positive tone.
- *Bless the Bills:* Like my ritual with Duncan, turn mundane tasks into gratitude moments. Paying a bill? Thank the service provider for what they've given you. Sending an email? Appreciate the technology connecting you to the world.
- *Gratitude on the Go:* Keep a small notebook or use your phone to jot down moments of joy throughout the day. A kind word from a coworker, a delicious lunch, a stranger's smile—these add up.
- *Evening Reflection:* Before bed, reflect on one thing that went well. Even on a rough day, there's something—a lesson, a laugh, a breath. These plant seeds of hope for tomorrow.
- *Share the Love:* Tell someone you're grateful for them. A quick text, a heartfelt note, or a hug can deepen your connections and amplify your joy.

BADASS PRACTICE:
THE POETIC POWER OF GRATITUDE

Gratitude is a song you sing to the universe, a melody that puts your soul in step with the world's rhythm. It's the whisper of thanks when the stars align and the shout when they don't, but you still find reasons to smile. It's kissing the envelope of a bill, not because you're flush with cash, but because you're rich in perspective. It's meeting a hero like Louise Hay and feeling your heart swell with appreciation for her light, knowing that it has sparked your own.

This practice isn't about perfection—it's about presence. It's standing in the mess of life and saying, "I see you, and I also see the good." That's badass. That's grace. That's the foundation of a life filled with happiness and success, built one grateful moment at a time.

So start today. Count your blessings, big and small. Say "Thank you" to the world, to yourself, to the people, and moments that light your way. Watch how this simple act transforms your life into a masterpiece of gratitude and grace.

“Be fearless in the pursuit of what sets your soul on fire.”

—Jennifer Lee, American filmmaker and playwright

The Art of the Reframe: From Glass Half Empty to Cup Overflowing

My friend Nina Lesowitz is the best at reframing of anyone I know. She is a major gratitude badass. I have learned more from her about the importance of thankfulness and reframing than anyone else. Her beautiful house burned down in a tragic California wildfire that devastated entire towns. I remember sorting through the ashes with her, and she was happy to find a few things that survived the blaze. A few years later, her marriage had also turned to ashes, and she was brokenhearted but also confident that better times were ahead. She was right—she met a wonderful man, and they have a blissful relationship, the happiest couple at any gathering. Every time life serves lemons to Nina, she makes gallons of delicious lemonade. Without fail! In her own wise words:

"In the midst of chaos or disappointing news, choosing to find something—anything—to be grateful for can spark a powerful shift. Practicing gratitude doesn't just lift your spirit; it can begin to transform your circumstances. It really is that powerful!" Nina's book, *Living Life as a Thank You*, is one I highly recommend to any badass who wants to up their gratitude game. Reframe your way to a happier future!

The art of the reframe is badass alchemy, transforming a glass half empty into a cup overflowing with possibility. It's not about denying life's challenges but about shifting your lens to see the abundance woven into every moment. Reframing is gratitude's bold cousin, a mindset that flips negativity into opportunity, scarcity into plenty. When you master this art, you don't just cope—you thrive, radiating joy, grace, and unstoppable energy.

I used to sulk over bills, seeing only dwindling dollars. Then, inspired by Louise Hay, I reframed: Each payment became a thank-you for electricity and water, life's essentials. Suddenly my scarcity mindset cracked open, and I saw provision, not loss. Reframing isn't ignoring reality; it's choosing to spotlight the good within it. That flat tire? A chance to slow down and notice the world. A tough day at work? A lesson in resilience. This shift pulls you out of negative spirals, replacing dread with curiosity: *What's the gift here?* It's like swapping a gray filter for a vibrant one—same scene, new brilliance.

Your attitude is the brushstroke that paints your reality. A glass-half-empty mindset breeds worry; a cup-overflowing mindset breeds wonder. Reframing takes practice, but it's a muscle that grows stronger with use. The result? A life where setbacks become setups for growth, and every moment hums with potential.

"The key to finding happiness in this life is realizing that the only way to overcome is to transcend; to find happiness in the simple pleasures, to master the art of just being."

—Brianna Wiest, bestselling author and journalist

Reframe Your Way to an Overflowing Cup

- *Pause and Pivot:* When negativity hits, pause. Ask, "What's one positive angle here?" A missed bus means time to enjoy the breeze.

- *Gratitude Anchor:* List three things you're thankful for daily. This grounds you in abundance, making reframing easier.

- *Flip the Script:* Turn "I failed" into "I learned." Rewrite complaints as opportunities to grow.

- *Celebrate Small Wins:* Reframe tiny victories—like making your bed—as evidence of your power to shape your day.

- *Speak Abundance:* Say aloud, "My cup overflows with possibility." Words shape reality—make yours bold and grateful.

Master the reframe and watch your life bloom. Your cup won't just fill—it will spill over with badass gratitude and joy.

Nurturing Yourself with Gratitude

Gratitude isn't just about thanking the world around you—it's also about thanking *yourself* and nurturing your own heart. When you use gratitude as a self-care practice, you're giving yourself permission to heal, grow, and bloom, even after the hardest storms. Gratitude supports your mental health, builds self-compassion, and helps you mend past wounds.

I discovered this a few years ago when I was struggling with anxiety. I felt like I was failing at everything, and my inner critic was loud. One night, I wrote in my journal, "I'm grateful for my courage to keep going, even when I'm scared." That small act of self-kindness quieted the noise in my head. It reminded me that I was enough, just as I am.

Nurturing yourself with gratitude is like wrapping your soul in a warm blanket. It's thanking yourself for your resilience, your laughter, and your ability to learn from mistakes. It ties into self-belief and affirmations—like saying, "I'm grateful for my strength, and I'm growing every day." This practice helps you heal from past hurts by focusing on what you've gained, not just what you've lost. It's a way to be gentle with yourself, to say, "I'm doing my best, and that's worth celebrating."

BADASS PRACTICE: THE BLESSING BOWL

Find a small, beautiful bowl and place it somewhere special, like your nightstand or desk. Gather a few crystals: citrine for joy, amethyst for peace, and rose quartz—which I like to call love in the form of a stone, perfect for self-love. Each time you do something good for yourself—like taking a walk, resting when you're tired, or speaking kindly to yourself—add a crystal to your Blessing Bowl. As you place it, say, "I'm grateful for this act of self-care." Watch your bowl fill with shimmering reminders of your self-love. At the end of the month, share this practice with a friend—gift them with a small crystal to start their own bowl, and swap stories about your self-care moments. You'll feel the warmth of self-compassion growing stronger.

Gratitude for yourself is the ultimate act of self-care. It's how you grow, heal, and shine brighter every day. What will you thank yourself for today?

Amazing Grace: Giving Thanks at Mealtime Is the Recipe for a Badass Life

Picture this: a table groaning under the weight of a feast—crispy roast chicken, buttery mashed potatoes, a rainbow of veggies, and a pie so gorgeous it deserves its own Instagram account. Your crew is gathered, forks at the ready, stomachs rumbling like a summer storm. But before anyone dives in, you pause. You say grace. And in that moment, something magical happens—the meal transforms into a sacred memory-making ritual that bonds everyone tighter than a bear hug. Here's why saying grace is the ultimate gratitude hack and how to make it modern, meaningful, and downright fun.

Saying grace isn't just for stiff Sunday dinners at Grandma's house. It's a chance to hit pause in our go-go-go world and soak in the moment. Whether it's a fancy holiday spread or a Tuesday-night taco fest, taking a beat to express gratitude elevates the meal from "yum" to "holy wow." It's like adding a sprinkle of fairy dust—it makes everything sparkle. When you say grace, you're not just thanking the universe for the food (props to the farmers, cooks, and delivery folks who made it happen). You're weaving a thread of connection between everyone at the table, creating autonomy that'll stick in your heart like a favorite song.

So how do you say grace in a way that feels fresh and not like you're reciting a dusty prayer from a bygone era? Easy—make it personal, make it real, and make it *you*.

You could start by inviting everyone to share one thing they're grateful for. It could be the crispy edges on the lasagna, the fact that your bestie made it through traffic to be there, or just the miracle of the Wi-Fi staying connected during dinner prep. If you're feeling fancy, light a candle or pass around a "gratitude stone" (yep, just a cool rock you keep on the table) to set the vibe. For a fun twist, try a gratitude freestyle—everyone tosses out a quick "Thank you" for something specific, like a round-robin rap battle of positivity. "Yo, I'm thankful for this mac and cheese; it's gonna make my heart say *please*!" Trust me, it'll spark giggles and warm fuzzies.

Why does this matter? Because saying grace turns a meal into a sacred moment. It's a reminder that food isn't just fuel—it's love, effort, and connection on a plate. When you pause to give thanks, you're not just eating; you're creating a memory. Think of those times you still laugh about—like when Uncle Joe spilled gravy during Thanksgiving grace or when your kiddo thanked "the pizza gods" with total sincerity. Those moments stick because they're infused with intention. They're the amber-trapped memories you'll carry forever.

Plus, grace is a bonding superpower. It levels the playing field—whether you're a CEO or a toddler, everyone gets to share what's in their heart. It's a chance to see each other, really *see* each other, beyond the daily grind. You might learn that your quiet cousin is grateful for her new puppy or that your grumpy neighbor secretly loves your homemade salsa. These shared snippets build trust, love, and a sense of "We're in this together."

So the next time you're about to dig in, don't skip grace. Make it fun, make it yours, and watch it transform your meal into a sacred, heartwarming, memorable celebration. Because a plate of gratitude? That's the real recipe for a badass life.

Gratitude in Love: Deepening Your Romantic Bond

Love is a beautiful, messy adventure, and gratitude can be the secret ingredient that makes it even sweeter. When you bring gratitude into your romantic relationship, you're not just saying "I love you"—you're saying, "I see you, I appreciate you, and I'm so thankful you're mine." This hit home for me last year when my partner and I were going through a rough patch. We were both stressed, barely connecting, and I could feel the distance growing. One evening, I decided to try something. I left a sticky note on his coffee mug that said, "I'm grateful for how you always make me laugh, even on hard days." When he saw it, his whole face lit up. He wrote one back: "I'm grateful for your endless support." That night, we talked for hours, really seeing each other again. Those little notes became our way of staying connected, and they brought us closer than ever.

Gratitude in love is about noticing the small things—like the way your partner makes your coffee just right, or how they hold your hand when you're nervous. It's also about appreciating the big stuff, like their unwavering support or the way they challenge you to grow. When you express gratitude, you're not just strengthening your bond; you're creating a safe space where love can flourish, even through the storms. It's a way to honor your partner's presence in your life, reminding you both why you chose each other in the first place.

BADASS PRACTICE:
THE LOVE GRATITUDE RITUAL

Set aside a few minutes each week to share gratitude with your partner. Sit together—maybe over a cozy dinner or a quiet morning coffee—and take turns saying one thing you're grateful for about each other. It could be "I'm thankful for how you listened to me this week," or "I'm grateful for your silly dance moves that make me smile." Write these statements of gratitude on a shared piece of paper or in a notebook you keep just for this ritual. Over time, you'll have a beautiful collection of love-filled moments to look back on. Then, extend the love outward: Share this practice with a couple you're close to, like your best friends, and encourage them to try it. You'll all feel the warmth of gratitude rippling through your relationships.

Gratitude doesn't fix every challenge in love, but it builds a foundation of appreciation that can weather any storm. It's a daily choice to say, "I'm thankful for us." So take a moment today to thank your partner for something small, something big, or something that makes your heart flutter. What will you celebrate about your love story today? You've got a love worth cherishing—let gratitude make it shine.

Six Tips for a Memorable, Magical Mealtime Grace

Saying grace before a meal is like hitting the "start" button on a joyful, soul-nourishing experience. It's not just about giving thanks—it's about weaving connection, sparking laughter, and making every bite feel like a celebration. Whether you're serving pizza on paper plates or a five-course feast, these six tips will make your grace a magical moment that sticks in everyone's heart, like a warm cookie fresh from the oven.

1. **KEEP IT SHORT AND SWEET:** Nobody wants a sermon when the mashed potatoes are calling. Aim for grace that's brief but heartfelt—thirty seconds to a minute, tops. Try something like "We're grateful for this food, the hands that made it, and the love around this table. Let's eat!" It's quick, punchy, and sets a joyful tone. For extra fun, end with a group cheer—think "Amen!" or "Chow time!"—to get everyone smiling.

2. **MAKE IT PERSONAL:** Ditch the one-size-fits-all prayers and tailor your grace to the moment.

Mention something specific: the friend who brought the killer guacamole, the fact that it's your kid's first day at school, or even the rainy day that made cozy soup night possible. Personal touches show everyone you're present, and it invites them to feel the gratitude too. Bonus: It's a memory anchor for that exact meal.

3. **INVITE EVERYONE TO JOIN IN:** Grace isn't a solo act—it's a group jam session. Ask each person to share one thing they're thankful for, like a gratitude relay. It could be the crispy tacos, a promotion at work, or just "this crew right here." For shy folks, keep it low pressure—pass a "gratitude spoon" (or any fun object) to signal whose turn it is. This inclusivity builds bonds and sparks stories you'll laugh about for years.

4. **ADD A DASH OF PLAYFULNESS:** Make grace fun to keep it fresh! Try a gratitude rhyme: "For food so fine and friends divine, let's eat and make this moment shine!" Or go for a themed grace—on taco night, thank the "salsa gods" for spicy perfection. For kids (or young-at-heart adults), add a silly ritual, like everyone tapping their plate twice for good luck. Playfulness turns grace into a moment everyone looks forward to.

5. **CREATE A SIGNATURE RITUAL:** Build a tradition that's uniquely yours to make grace a memory-maker. Maybe you light a candle to signal the start, hold hands for a quick squeeze, or clink glasses afterward. My friends and I once started passing a tiny ceramic heart around the table—each person said a quick "Thanks" while holding it. Years later, we still talk about "the heart nights." Your ritual doesn't have to be fancy—just consistent enough to feel like home.

6. **REFLECT THE SEASON OR VIBE:** Tie your grace to the moment's energy. In autumn, thank the harvest and cozy sweater weather. On a random Tuesday, give a shout-out to surviving the workweek. For big gatherings, acknowledge the effort it took to get everyone together. This grounds the moment, making it feel sacred and connected to the bigger picture. Pro tip: If it's a holiday, weave in a nod to its spirit—like gratitude for freedom on the Fourth of July.

These tips turn grace into a magical glue that binds your table, making every meal a chance to connect, laugh, and create memories. So the next time you gather, sprinkle in some gratitude, add a pinch of fun, and watch your meal become a moment no one forgets. Here's to plates full of love and hearts full of badass gratitude!

A Badass Guide to Crafting a Vision Board That Sparks Magic

Ready to turn your dreams into a gratitude-charged reality? A vision board is your ticket to manifesting a life that's as bold and beautiful as you are. Here are eight tips for creating a vision board that's equal parts inspiration, motivation, and pure *Badass Gratitude* magic—perfect for keeping your goals front and center and your heart full of fire.

1. **Dream Big, Then Get Specific:** Start by letting your imagination run wild—think beach villas, world travel, or that dream job where you're the boss of your own destiny. Then, get specific. Want a new career? Pin a photo of your ideal office or a phrase like "CEO vibes only." This combo of big dreams and clear details gives your vision board focus and purpose. Grab a journal and jot down what lights you up before you start cutting and pasting. Gratitude hack: Thank the universe for these dreams as if *they're* already yours. It's like sending a cosmic RSVP to your future.
2. **Make It a Gratitude Party:** Turn vision-board creation into a celebration! Invite your besties, crank up a playlist of feel-good jams, and pour some tea (or something bubblier). As you flip through magazines, share what you're grateful for—maybe it's your crew, your courage, or even that perfect latte you had this

morning. This grateful vibe infuses your board with love and makes the process a memory you'll cherish. Pro tip: Add a group gratitude ritual, like everyone shouting one thing they're thankful for before you start gluing. It's a bonding moment that makes your board *extra* magical.

3. **Curate Your Visuals with Intention:** Every image, quote, or trinket on your board should scream *you*. Hunt for visuals that spark joy—a sunny beach for your dream vacay, a sleek laptop for your side hustle, or a heart-shaped doodle for love. Don't just slap on random pics; choose ones that make your heart do a happy dance. Gratitude twist: As you add each item, say a quick "Thank you" for the step it represents toward your goal. This keeps your energy high and your board a true reflection of your badass aspirations.
4. **Keep It Visible and Vibrant:** Your vision board isn't a "make it and forget it" deal. Place it where you'll see it daily—by your desk, above your bed, or even as your phone's wallpaper. This constant reminder keeps your goals front and center, like a gratitude-fueled cheerleader. Refresh it every few months with new images or quotes to match your evolving dreams.
5. **Gratitude Hack:** Each time you glance at it, say, "I'm so thankful for how close I'm getting!" This keeps the

motivation flowing and turns your board into a living, breathing part of your journey.

6. **Add a Playful Flair:** Make your board as fun as a barrel of glitter-dipped monkeys! Use bright colors, stickers, or even a sprinkle of actual glitter (because why not?). Write sassy affirmations such as "I'm a money-magnet badass," or "Adventure awaits me!" in a bold marker. For extra fun, add a tiny toy car for that dream ride or a mini heart for self-love.
7. **Gratitude Spin:** Thank your creative spirit for making the process a blast. This playful energy keeps your board from feeling like a chore and turns it into an inspirational ritual that sparks joy.
8. **Reflect and Act with Gratitude:** A vision board isn't just eye candy—it's a call to action. Each week, spend a moment with your board, reflecting on your progress. Ask, "What's one step I can take toward this goal?" Maybe it's signing up for a class or saving $20 for that dream trip.

Gratitude boost: Thank yourself for every action you take, no matter how small. This keeps you grounded in the present while moving toward your future. Your board becomes a gratitude-powered guide, reminding you that every step is a victory in your badass journey to a dream-filled life.

"Do not ignore your intuition. There is an infinite intelligence within you; let it be your guiding light."

—Cleo Wade, bestselling American poet, author, artist, and activist

Vision Board: Your Badass Blueprint for a Dream-Charged Life

Picture this: You're standing in front of a blank canvas, armed with a stack of magazines, a glue stick, and a heart full of dreams so big they could light up the San Francisco skyline. This, my friend, is your vision board—a magical glitter-dusted road map to the life you're itching to live. It's not just a craft project; it's a gratitude-fueled rocket ship that launches your goals from "Someday" to "Heck yeah, today!" A vision board transforms your life by turning your wildest aspirations into a visual party that keeps you focused, fired up, and ready to slay.

Creating a vision board is like throwing a gratitude bash for your future self. You snip out images of that dream beach house, that killer career, or that epic road trip across Route 66, and suddenly, your goals aren't just fuzzy ideas—they're *real*. Every glance at your board is a high-five to your dreams, reminding you why you're hustling through traffic or burning the midnight oil. It's clarity in Technicolor, helping you ditch the noise of daily life and zero in on what makes your soul sing.

But here's the real magic: A vision board is like a gratitude-powered magnet. By visualizing your goals—whether it's a cozy cabin or a marathon finish line—you're telling the universe, "This is my vibe!" It's the Law of Attraction with a side of sass, pulling opportunities your way like confetti to a dance floor. And let's not forget the motivation factor. On those days when you're ready to hide under the covers with a pint of ice cream, your vision board is there whispering, "You got this, badass." It's a daily dose of inspiration that keeps you pushing through challenges, a gratitude-fueled superhero.

Plus, making a vision board is just plain *fun*. It's a chance to get messy with glitter glue, sip tea with your besties, and dream big without judgment. It's a stress-busting, heart-lifting ritual that turns your hopes into a tangible masterpiece. And every time you look at it, you're reminded of the life you're building—one bold, grateful step at a time. So grab those scissors, channel your inner artist, and create a vision board that screams, "This is my dream, and I'm making it happen!" Because with a little gratitude and a lot of vision, you're unstoppable.

Journal Your Way to a Life of Badass Gratitude: Unlocking Joy, Purpose, and Deep Self-Insight

Grab a notebook, and let's turn a blank page into a doorway to joy, purpose, and a deeper understanding of yourself. Journaling isn't just jotting down thoughts; it's a powerful, transformative act that rewires your mind, opens your heart, and invites new blessings into your life. This isn't about forcing yourself to write a chore list or churning out a feel-good diary. It's about owning your story, finding gratitude in the mess, and uncovering insights that make you feel like you're living with intention.

When I started journaling during my lean days in San Francisco, scraping by on apples and potatoes, it became my way of saying, "I'm still here, and I'm thankful for it." That practice turned my struggles into stepping stones and my gratitude into fuel for a better life. Here's how to journal your way to a life filled with badass gratitude, joy, and purpose—without it feeling like a grind. Get ready to meet yourself on the page and watch new doors open.

Journaling for gratitude is a daily nod to your inner strength. It's not about ignoring life's tough moments or pretending everything's perfect—it's about finding the small sparks of good and letting them grow. Think of it as a treasure hunt: Every entry uncovers moments of joy, lessons from pain, and clues to who you are at your core. The goal? To build a mindset that doesn't just get by but thrives, drawing blessings and opportunities toward you like a magnet. Back in my Haight Street days, journaling helped me see beyond the struggle. I'd write about a kind word from a stranger or a quiet moment watching the fog roll in. Those weren't just nice—they were proof that I was still in the fight, and they fueled my drive. By putting pen to paper, you're not just reflecting; you're reshaping your story to make room for joy, purpose, and insights that light your path.

The beauty of gratitude journaling is that it's not a task—it's a vibe. It's a chance to get real with yourself, smile at your quirks, and celebrate your wins, no matter how small. It's having a heart-to-heart with your best self, where you can say, "I'm proud of you for getting through that tough day," or "I'm thankful for my quirky neighbor's loud jazz because it reminds me that life's never dull." This practice deepens your understanding of yourself, helping you notice patterns, dreams, and truths you might have missed otherwise.

And the best part? It's a blessings magnet. When you focus on gratitude, you start seeing more to be grateful for—new connections, unexpected possibilities, and doors you didn't know were there. So grab a notebook, a favorite pen, or even a scrap of paper, and let's dive into six tips to make journaling your key to a life full of badass gratitude.

Six Tips to Journal Your Way to Badass Gratitude

1. **Start with a Meaningful Prompt:** Begin each entry with a question that sparks reflection or joy. Try "What made me feel strong today?" or "What's one thing that went right, even if it was small?" This isn't about forcing gratitude—it's about finding it in your own way. During my broke days, I'd ask, "What kept me going today?" One time, it was a free coffee from a coworker. That small moment became a lifeline. Write for two to three minutes, and let the answers surprise you. This sets the tone for joy and helps you notice blessings you might've overlooked.
2. **Use Gratitude Lists for Quick Wins:** Lists are an easy way to capture gratitude fast. Write "Three Things

I'm Thankful for" or "Five Moments That Felt Good This Week" (even if it's just "I didn't lose my keys"). Include big and small moments—your friend's laugh, a cozy blanket, or finishing a tough task. I once listed "potatoes, because they got me through" and smiled at the memory. It's not about perfection; it's about noticing what lifts you up. Lists train your mind to spot joy, making purpose feel closer and new opportunities easier to see.

3. **Get Honest with Freewriting:** Set a timer for five minutes and write whatever comes up—no filter, no editing. Pour out frustrations, hopes, or random thanks for your dog's goofy energy. This is where deep self-insight lives. When I freewrote during hard times, I'd start with "I'm so tired of this" and end up grateful for my resilience. Don't hold back; just let it flow. This honesty uncovers truths about yourself and clears mental space for unexpected blessings.
4. **Reframe the Tough Moments:** Life isn't always easy, and your journal should reflect that. When things get rough, write about it, then shift your perspective. Ask, "What did this challenge teach me?" or "What's still good, even in this mess?" After a tough move, I journaled about the stress but found gratitude for the chance to start fresh. This isn't about ignoring pain—it's about finding strength in it. Reframing

builds purpose from chaos and opens doors to growth you didn't expect.

5. **Celebrate Your Strengths:** Dedicate entries to cheering yourself on. Write about a time you showed up, felt proud, or helped someone. Try "I'm proud of myself because..." or "I showed my strength when..." I once wrote, "I'm proud for carrying recycling bags in a suit like a champ." It's not boasting—it's owning your value. This boosts joy, deepens understanding of yourself, and attracts opportunities by reminding you how capable you are.
6. **End with a Gratitude Power Statement:** Close each session with a bold gratitude note: "I'm thankful for [X] because it's leading me to [Y]." Example: "I'm thankful for my persistence because it's opening doors to new possibilities." This ties gratitude to purpose, making it a launchpad for blessings. I'd end entries with "I'm thankful for this city's energy because it's teaching me to thrive anywhere." It's a strong way to wrap up and keep your focus on the doors opening ahead.

Why It Works

These tips make journaling a joy, not a burden, because they're flexible, honest, and personal. They meet you where you are—whether you're soaring or struggling—

and turn gratitude into a habit that sparks joy, purpose, and insight. Each entry helps you understand your incredible self better and invites blessings, from stronger connections to new opportunities. So pick up that pen, get real, and watch your life light up with gratitude that opens doors you never knew were there.

A Thank-You That Heals

Sometimes, life leaves little cracks in your heart—maybe a friendship faded or a dream didn't pan out. I get it; I've been there. A few years back, I lost touch with my best friend from high school after a silly misunderstanding. I missed her laugh, our late-night talks, and the way she'd hype me up. I was hurt, but I decided to try something: I wrote her a thank-you note. Not to fix things, but to honor what we'd had. "Thank you for all the memories," I wrote. "They still make me smile." I mailed it, and a week later, she called. We cried, laughed, and started rebuilding.

That's the magic of badass gratitude—it can heal. Saying "Thank you" doesn't erase the pain, but it softens it, like a warm hug for your soul. It helps you focus on the love that was there, not just the loss. And it opens doors to reconnect, even if it's just with your own heart.

BADASS PRACTICE: THE HEALING NOTE

Take a moment today to think of someone you've lost touch with or a situation that still stings. Write a short thank-you note—maybe to them or just for yourself. It could be "Thank you for the lessons," or "Thank you for the good times." If you feel ready, share it. If not, tuck it away. Either way, you're giving gratitude space to mend what's broken.

You're stronger than you know, and gratitude can be your bridge back to peace. Who can you thank today to start healing?

"Believe in yourself and what you feel. Your power will come from that."

—Melissa Lou Etheridge, award-winning American singer, songwriter, and guitarist

"Don't tear yourself down when you have the power to build yourself up."

—Chanel Miller, American writer, artist, and sexual-assault-victim advocate

BADASS PRACTICE: LIVE YOUR VALUES

When we are on track, living close to the things we deem important—the things we value—we feel happier. This isn't flash happiness; it isn't the kind that lasts for a few minutes, like when we get a new toy or enjoy a concert. This is the kind that lingers in the background of our lives. The kind that, even in moments of sadness or frustration, never completely disappears—because if we are living a values-based life, we are also living with meaning and purpose.

AFFIRMATION STATION

All I envision is in my reach.

My dreams are not distractions—
they are directions.

Gratitude informs my past,
fuels my present, and maps my future.

Every blessing I count builds
a stronger version of me.

CONCLUSION

Living Life as a Thank-You

Dear Reader, as we close the pages of *Badass Gratitude*, my heart is full of appreciation for you. You've walked this journey with me, embracing the wild, beautiful chaos of life and discovering how gratitude can transform even the toughest moments. Your willingness to explore, reflect, and open your heart to this practice is nothing short of inspiring. Thank you for trusting these words, for showing up, and for choosing to weave gratitude into the fabric of your life. This book isn't just about moments of thanks—it's about living with a grateful heart, day in and day out. You've learned to find light in the shadows, to nurture your spirit, and to strengthen the bonds that make life rich. As you move forward, I hope you carry this mindset with you, seeing every challenge and joy as a chance to say, "Thank you." Gratitude isn't just a practice; it's a way of being that can light up your path to a happy, fulfilled life. My deepest wish for you is that this journey continues to unfold with grace and courage. May you find peace in the small moments, strength in the hard ones, and joy in the connections you cherish. You are already a badass, and with gratitude as your guide, there's no limit to the beauty you'll create in your life. Keep shining, keep growing, and keep saying "thank you" to the universe for all it brings your way. XO

Acknowledgments

Huge thank you to the amazing Kirsty Melville and her excellent Andrews McMeel team who transformed my idea into a stunningly beautiful object, one I will be proud of forever. My editor, Kate Zimmermann is the soul of patience and an awesome craftswoman; together with Julie Railsback, they turned an overabundance of words into a gift of gratitude. Designer Julie Barnes created a work of art and Julie Skalla's production made it the kind of book writers dream of. Brava!

About the Author

Becca Anderson comes from a long line of preachers and teachers from Ohio and Kentucky. The teacher side of her family led her to become a woman's studies scholar and the author of *The Book of Awesome Women*. An avid collector of meditations, prayers, and blessings, she helps run a "Gratitude and Grace Circle" that meets monthly at homes, churches, and bookstores in the San Francisco Bay Area where she currently resides. Becca Anderson credits her spiritual practice with helping her recover from cancer and wants to share this with anyone who is facing difficulty in their life.

Author of *Think Happy to Stay Happy, Every Day Thankful*, and the bestselling *Badass Affirmations*, Becca Anderson shares her inspirational writings and suggested acts of kindness at thedailyinspoblog.wordpress.com. She also blogs about Awesome Women at theblogofawesomewomen.wordpress.com.